Heavenly Life

by

Robert F. Simms

Copyright @2014 by Robert F. Simms
All rights reserved. No portion of this book may be reproduced or transmitted in any form by any means, electronic or mechanical, including photocopying, recording, or by any information storage retrieval system without permission from the author, except for brief quotations embodies in articles or reviews. All quotations of scripture except where noted otherwise come from the Authorized King James Version of the Bible.

ISBN: 978-0-9858233-4-4
Published in the United States by
Robert F. Simms
Greer, South Carolina

Contents

1

GOING TO HEAVEN 1
A Progressive Revelation in Words 3
Style of this Study 7

2

ORIGIN AND NATURE OF HEAVEN 9
A Created Place 9
A Spiritual Place 11
A Specific Place 17

3

WHO IS IN HEAVEN? 23
God the Father 23
God the Son 27
Angels 30
Old Testament Saints 32
The Born-Again in Christ 37
Unaccountable Children 47

4

WHY IS THERE A HEAVEN? 53
Object of Instinctive Longing 53
Answer to Mysteries of Life 55
Justice for All 57
The Present Purpose 60

5

HEAVEN ON EARTH 73
Earth and Heaven Re-created 74
Life without Sorrow or Death 83
Freedom, Perfection and Wholeness 94

6
- THE NEW JERUSALEM 98
- John's Revealing Vision 98
- Heaven's Geography 109

7
- HEAVEN, GOD'S VICTORY 117
- Causes of Skepticism 117
- Reasons for Revising Our Beliefs 121

8
- OUR LIVES IN HEAVEN 124
- Bodily but Not Sexual 124
- Unchanged for Eternity 130
- Like Jesus 133

9
- A DAY IN HEAVEN 141

APPENDIX
- ABBREVIATIONS OF BIBLE BOOKS 147

I
Going to Heaven

Around the world, in every culture, in every country, throughout human history, probably the greatest yearning of human beings has been to know that a heaven exists and that they will go there when they die. Religions in all times and places have postulated that man is more than the body we see in the physical world. When people died, other people around them believed that there was an essence to them that continued to exist; therefore, it was a natural and logical conclusion that there was some place or state into which the spiritual or invisible essence went.

The idea of heaven in the oldest and major religions varies: from a state of idyllic oneness with the divine being, with a merging of the individual personality into that of a universal spirit; to a nirvana where heaven is a divine mental state achieved through reincarnation and acquisition of positive karma; to a realm virtually the same as this visible world, but perfected in every way and with multiplied riches and pleasures; to an ethereal existence mostly devoid of tangible experiences, consisting principally of emotional and spiritual happiness and contentment; and to a dimension of existence in which human beings know each other as before and are able to see and know their Creator, in an atmosphere of perfect and joyful living.

Every religion has its own literature describing heaven along with other tenets of that faith. The sacred writings usually claim to be based on the inspired thoughts of highly revered persons, sometimes the recounting of these persons' visions of divine beings and places, and occasionally the dictation or direct transmission of authoritative material from beyond.

Adding to the general, cultural belief in heaven are the stories of many people claiming to have experienced a brief time in heaven and to have returned. Known widely today as NDEs (Near Death Experiences), these claimed encounters often mention tunnels emerging into bright lights, loved ones waiting on the other side, a presence identified as God, and figures recognized as Jesus, angels, or other religious persons. In some of these stories, people have reported facing a review of their lives, reaching a final barrier beyond which return to this life is impossible, and being given the choice to go back or not, or being told that they must. Records of NDEs are at least as old as the 4th century B.C. Some of the more recent NDEs include extensive accounts published with the intention of proving the existence of heaven and telling people in this world how to guarantee their entrance into heaven at the time of death.

Philosophers and thinkers of all kinds, and students of the various sacred writings of world religions, have added to the literature about heaven with commentaries on what their scriptures say. A compendium, even a concise one, on what the peoples of the world have believed heaven would be like would be a weighty volume, and studying it would necessarily be an academic pursuit. This book, on the other hand, is intended to be a specific study in what the Bible says about heavenly life.

This study is meant for Christians and for those who may be attracted to the Christian faith. Its purpose is to help the reader discover how the many diverse references and discussions of heaven throughout the Bible come together to give a picture of what the Christian may expect to experience when life in this present world comes to a close. The expectation of heaven is truly universal. The Bible offers what Christians believe is God's own revelation of the truth about heaven, to the extent that human beings need to know of it while in this world.

A Progressive Revelation in Words

This book will not make any attempt at a thorough study of the ancient languages involved in the biblical texts. Non-scholars—which most of us are—generally prefer only as much background study as is necessary to explain the heart of an issue. We will limit our study of the Hebrew of the Old Testament and the Greek of the New Testament to a depth that sufficiently supports our discovery of the essential meaning of the biblical texts. The ancient languages will be represented by commonly accepted English transliterations.

The biblical Hebrew and Greek use different words to convey facets of thought about heaven. In a general way, these words carry the Bible reader from Genesis to Revelation in a progressive uncovering of a fuller and fuller depiction of man's universal longing.

Here are the major Hebrew words appearing in the biblical texts:

shamayim

This Hebrew word is used in the plural form (the "-im" ending) to refer to heights or elevations. It is the word used in Gen 1:1 and 2:2 where God created and finished "the heavens and the earth." From early in the history of the Hebrew people, they conceived of three levels of the heavens: the first heaven, the immediate sky where the birds fly and clouds float; the second heaven, known as the firmament, where the stars and other heavenly bodies exist; and the third heaven, which is the abode of God, angels, and those who go from this world to be with God.

marom

This word means high places or heights. It is used in Psa 68:18, "Thou hast ascended on high;" Psa 93:4, "The LORD on high;" and Psa 102:19, "The height of his sanctuary." It indicates that the heaven referred to is the third heaven.

shahak

Meaning "sky," this word was employed by Moses in Deu 33:26 to describe the LORD who "rideth upon the heaven in thy help." The word may indicate the first heaven where God may control weather in favor of his people, or it may refer to the third heaven where he rules in a sovereign way over human events. Job used *shahak* in 37:18 to refer to the sky, and Psa 18:11 and other scriptures employ the word to mean simply the skies.

rakia

This word means "firmament," a reference to the Hebrew second heaven, and appears in Gen 1:6, Deu 33:26 and other places. The firmament was apparently conceived of as a solid dome, separating the earth from the third heaven.

Here are the major Greek words used in the New Testament to indicate heaven:

ouranos

Most references to heaven in the New Testament are this word *ouranos,* which is translated simply "heaven" and depends on its context for what exactly it depicts. Generally, it means a place lifted up, i.e., from the earth, where God, angels and saints live. It appears in Mat 3:17 where "lo, a voice from heaven" proclaimed Jesus to be God's beloved Son. It is used in Mat 5:12 to refer to "reward in heaven." Matthew 6:1 employs the word in describing "your Father which is in heaven," and in Mat 6:20 where Jesus describes laying up "treasures in heaven," *ouranos* is the word the gospel writer used. Elsewhere in the New Testament, the phrase, "the kingdom of heaven," uses this same word for heaven. Mar 13:32 uses *ouranos* to tell where the angels are. In Luk 9:54, James and John want to call down "fire from heaven." In Joh 6:42, Jesus said "I came down from heaven." Act 7:55 says Stephen "looked up stedfastly into heaven and saw the glory of God." Paul's reference to the "third heaven" in 1Co 12:2 used the word *ouranos*. John likewise used the word in Rev 3:12 to describe the place out of which the New Jerusalem in his vision descended. Throughout Revelation, John used this Greek word to describe the place God dwells, the place from which history is being directed, and the place where the Father, Son and Spirit will reign in eternity, as well as the abode of those who "overcome by the blood of the Lamb" (Rev 12:11).

basileia

Besides the heavily used word *ouranos*, the Greek writers sometimes employed *basileia*, meaning "kingdom," to refer to heaven. While "the kingdom of heaven" usually refers to the general rule of God, both here and in his abode, *basileia* is used alone in verses such as Mat 4:23 to describe "the gospel of the kingdom." "Gospel" means good news, and the phrase "gospel of the kingdom" refers not only to the gospel as it affects life on earth, but the good news that admits persons into heaven when they respond to that news with acceptance and faith. Mat 16:28 uses *basileia* to describe "the Son of Man coming in his kingdom," a reference to the ultimate event of Christ's reign. The mother of Jesus' disciples James and John asked Jesus to grant that they might sit on the right and left "in your kingdom," another use of *basileia*. The thief on the cross who repented asked Jesus to remember him "when thou comest into thy kingdom," and Paul, in 1Co 6:10, spoke of Christians who "inherit the kingdom." All these references point to the dwelling place of God and saints, emphasizing the fact that God rules there perfectly and fully.

All in all, there are 249 references in the New Testament alone to the exact word, "heaven," not counting "heavens" or "heavenly." Of these, 85 references are to heaven as God's dwelling place. The idea of a kingdom of heaven takes up another 35 references, and there are 23 references to heaven as the dwelling place of saints, the people of God.

Various other words describe attributes of heaven, and we will bring those words into the discussion along the way in this study.

The words used for heaven throughout the Bible and the context of those words in the stories or teachings where they appear constitute a body of material that is rich and picturesque. The variety alone suggests strongly that it is possible for us to put together a fairly complete picture of eternal life and heaven, at least to the extent that we need to know it. At the same time, the Bible has given us much more information than most people have ever either assembled or assimilated into their theology. Putting together the biblical descriptions in a logical and theologically defensible way enables us to connect the dots, so to speak, or to color in what has only been outlined. Then incorporating our discoveries about heaven with our other biblical beliefs about salvation, Christ, death and other doctrines, will enable us to imagine our future realistically.

Style of this Study

Our study will be described by several adjectives:

Investigative

We will try to look behind Bible verses to the background thought and cultural assumptions that shape the authors' uses of their terms. Our goal will be to avoid presumption or *eisigesis* (reading our understanding back into an earlier writer's words) and to grasp what the original Bible authors meant when they spoke of heaven.

Deductive

We will attempt to allow scripture to lead us to likely conclusions about heaven that are consistent with other scriptures. This method of using other Bible passages to interpret scripture ensures that we do not isolate a verse from its context, either its immediate setting or that of the whole Bible.

Open and Non-dogmatic

While we will reach some firm interpretations and conclusions, we will try to avoid the kind of inflexibility that derives from pride and self-assurance, and that divides Christians from one another on doctrinal issues. We will discover that many of the Bible's references to heaven are suggestive rather than explicit. This fact alone will serve to moderate any desire we might have to arrive at a hard and fixed position on the characteristics of heaven. Our goal is to develop an interpretation that inspires and enlightens.

With these hopeful characteristics of our study, we launch our little journey into what the Bible has to say about the place human beings of all time have wanted to go.

2
Origin and Nature of Heaven

"In the beginning," says Gen 1:1, "God created the heavens and the earth."

A Created Place

The Hebrew concept of three heavens was already developed at the point of this writing, which was somewhere around 1,400 to 1,500 years before Christ, or about 3,500 years ago. The Bible does not give a date for the creation of everything or an age of the universe. Whenever that was, however, the opening verse of Genesis declares that both the physical universe that we can observe and God's own dwelling place were brought into being. Heaven, as a place where God and angels dwell, did not always exist.

We should not worry ourselves with the human notion of God's being "homeless" in the absence of heaven as his dwelling. The God of the Bible is self-existent, sufficient unto himself and needing nothing to complete him. Think of his creating heaven as we might build our first home after leaving the home of our parents. While we were not homeless before, building a home was an expression of our creativity and an outworking of our plans for our future. Genesis shows us God making the physical world as an outworking of his creative nature and for his dramatic, sovereign purposes. Along with that physical reality, God created a place with which he could be identified, and where human beings would come to understand that he and the angels dwelled, and where many human beings themselves would live someday.

The concept of heaven as being above us is casually suggested in the words used in the Old Testament and the New. Even today, most of us are more comfortable being able to point to where things are rather than to wax eloquent on the niceties of physics and talk about alternate universes or inter-dimensional space. The ancient Hebrews quite naturally developed a concept of heaven's being above them. Their lack of complex scientific information obviated any other option. We'll look at this concept more later.

Neh 9:6 validates the conclusion that Gen 1:1 and 2:1 say that God created his own dwelling place. "You alone are the LORD," says Nehemiah, "You made the heavens, even the highest heavens [third heaven], and all their starry host, the earth and all that is on it, the seas and all that is in them. You give life to everything, and the multitudes of heaven worship you." God made his own house and the creatures who dwell in it. Nothing exists that God did not make. Even if we look at the creation as a bursting forth of energy into what became an eventual universe of billions of galaxies and worlds, the Bible's firm words are that God's creative power and genius are the answer to the question of where everything came from. This includes the heaven we hope to go to.

New Testament passages also confirm the created nature of heaven. Paul said that God was the architect and builder of heaven. "For we know that if our earthly house of this tabernacle were dissolved," wrote the Apostle, "we have a building of God, an house not made with hands, eternal in the heavens" (2Co 5:1). This verse may refer as much to the form our own lives will take in heaven as it does to heaven itself, but the terminology seems more fitted to a description of a structure or place than it does to what form our heavenly bodies might take. Comparing what Paul wrote to what Jesus said in the Gospel of John about preparing places for his disciples so they could be with him, we are probably safe in saying that Paul was referring not only to heaven as a general place created by God but also to individual dwellings where people will make their homes there.

This idea suggests broadly but firmly that heaven is not a vast throne room where people are gathered in endless corporate worship, but rather a place of limitless variety, beauty and interest as well as security.

A Spiritual Place

As opposed to this present world, which we commonly call physical, heaven is a spiritual place. This means some things we have commonly associated with the word but it doesn't mean some of the things people have connected with it from other contexts.

Indications from Scripture

John the Apostle, who as an old man was banished to the Isle of Patmos, wrote about his visions there, revelations uniquely delivered to him from Jesus Christ personally. His experience clearly was something most Christians would long to have. In Rev 4:2, John said, "At once I was in the Spirit, and there before me was a throne in heaven with someone sitting on it." John's being "in the Spirit" implies the general setting of what he observed was the spiritual realm.

Jesus described God as "Spirit," as opposed to an enormous, physical being somewhere concealed from human eyes. We rightly describe the nature of heaven as relating closely to the nature of God, which is spiritual.

Paul related an incident told to him by another Christian.

" I know a man in Christ who fourteen years ago was caught up to the third heaven," he wrote in 2Co 12:2-4. "Whether it was in the body or out of the body I do not know—God knows. And I know that this man—whether in the body or apart from the body I do not know, but God knows—was caught up to paradise. He heard inexpressible things, things that man is not permitted to tell." Paul was careful to repeat that he was not making any assumption about the actual experience of the man. "In the body" may mean that the man was looking at heaven from the perspective of this physical world, not really in heaven, but peering through a divinely fashioned portal into things beyond. "Out of the body" may mean that the man might have actually received a temporary spiritual form in which to experience the glories of heaven, before being returned to his physical body. If these were the options, Paul was careful to tell his readers that he had no position on just what this greatly blessed person was experiencing when he saw heaven.

If the man were "out of the body," i.e. out of *this* body, then he was in a spiritual place rather than this physical one. Paul thus validated the genuine nature of the experience of the man he was telling us about. That person's experience taught us generally that heaven ("the third heaven") is the same as "paradise" (v.4). No internal evidence in this verse suggests that Paul's term, "third heaven" in v.2 and his word, "paradise" in v.4 are different at all. So, references to paradise are about heaven.

Paul's having related this account from his friend, even if it were the only such story in scripture (which it isn't) by itself provides a foundation for our accepting the credibility of some of the stories Christians over the centuries have told about having had encounters with things in heaven, people in heaven, and even God. Whether by dreams (in the body?) or visions (in the body? out of the body?) or through NDEs, it is clear that Christians are not to discount the possibility that rare individuals have glimpsed heaven in some way.

A discussion of human experiences of heaven from this side of death is not our purpose. Evaluating the reports of such encounters would take volumes. In general, we should note simply that while the Bible itself lays the foundation for the possibility and existence of genuine encounters of human beings on this side with the spiritual heaven on the other side, every story of such an encounter must meet the test of consistency with biblical teaching. If a story of an NDE, for instance, departs from the Bible's clear teaching about the gospel, salvation exclusively through Jesus Christ alone, or any other firmly taught biblical truth, the account should be rejected as being something other than a true glimpse of God's heaven.

Nature of Spiritual Things

To say that heaven is a spiritual place as opposed to a physical one is not to diminish the reality of spiritual things or realms. Here is where many people make a serious conceptual mistake. Throughout the millennia of human existence, people have conceived of the spirits of human beings as ghosts, ethereal entities not quite real. The realm where spirits reside has been thought to be similarly ghostly, intangible, like a vapor or smoke. Ghost stories regularly suggest that spirits and the spiritual realm are more like images than objects, that there is no substance to things and people there. Not only would our own hands pass through these ghosts, but perhaps they are like holograms even to themselves. This is a fictional concept that does not comport with the Bible.

It is true that some people described in the Bible believed

in ghosts. The disciples when they saw Jesus walking on the water were terrified, thinking he was a spirit. They may have meant a *demonic* spirit, but more likely they thought he was a human being's spirit, what most people mean when they say "ghost." In 1Sa 28, Saul attempted to have a witch conjure up the dead prophet Samuel for advice, and some spirit did appear. The most reliable interpreters hold that it was a demonic spirit, who gave an accurate prophecy, but for the purpose of depressing Saul to the point of hopelessness. The bottom line for our study is that human beings who die do not become what the world commonly describes as ghosts.

The suggestion that "spiritual" implies "unreal" does a tremendous disservice to biblical teaching about spiritual beings, which all of us are, as well as being physical ones. The fact that our spiritual natures are invisible *to us* does not mean that they are less real or have no form or substance. It merely means that our physical bodies *in this physical realm* cannot touch our spirits or those of others, or perceive them in the way that we can touch and feel things in the physical world we see with our bodily eyes. Every indication we have of the spiritual realm, however, is that people in it are quite real to one another and to the things in that realm.

Paul's description of his friend in 2Co 12:2 as having been caught up to the third heaven "whether in the body or out of the body" implies that this person either was in *this body*, the body that Paul knew as his friend, or wasn't in *this body,* but out of it and in some form through which he could experience things in heaven. Paul wasn't saying that his friend was reduced to an unreal state, but rather that his spiritual nature may have been temporarily released from this body in order to have the full experience of another realm, a realm we commonly call the spiritual one.

Nothing in the Bible about spiritual places or entities is

ever presented as unreal, or less real, or even less *substantial* than the world with which we are most familiar by sight, sound and touch.

The Bible even connects the concepts of the body and spirit to teach us about the nature of spiritual entities. In 1Co 15:44, Paul talked about the certainty of the resurrection of saints and asserted without question that the spiritual realm has its own kind of corporeal reality. "It is sown a natural body," he said, speaking of burial, and "it is raised a spiritual body. If there is a natural body, there is also a spiritual body."

Paul was trying to communicate the idea of the spiritual realm's having a *substance* of its own kind, not the same as the substance or the material world we now see, but no less real than this one.

Modern astrophysics has contributed to our mathematical and conceptual grasp of the existence and reality of other realms. The old and familiar science fiction idea of other dimensions of time and space has a solid foundation in actual theories of physics. Current theories are that there may be not merely one or two other dimensions but limitless ones. What is known as the theory of multiverses (many universes) postulates that what produced our own universe may have produced an infinite number of other ones as well. According to this theory, while no one and nothing in the universe, the galaxy, the solar system, and the planet we know ourselves to be in, can see or touch or perceive in any way the things that are in any of these other universes, each of them is just as real as ours. We may exist in the same space, or we may each have our own space and time, independent of each other.

To put this concept back into the language of the Bible, even if we reduce the number of universes to only two, we might suggest that 'In the beginning, God created the heavens and the earth—the spiritual universe where he and the angels regularly live, and the physical universe where we live.'

What throws us off in our thinking about the corporeality of the spiritual realm is not only the fiction that has devolved around the fact that we cannot see our own spiritual natures, but the language we have used to describe our world.

- We say our world is "physical," which tends to imply that other things are not physical. In fact, if there are other universes, or if there is only one other universe and it is God's heaven, that universe must also be physical in the absolute sense. People there are real and objects exist just as they do here.
- We describe our world as "tangible," implying that the spiritual realm is not tangible, perhaps even to itself.

Thinking about the reality of the spiritual realm may be confused further by our acknowledging, in biblical terms, that human beings consist of body and spirit—the first which we see, and the second which we don't. Actually, to reference the tripartite concept of 1Th 5:23, we are body, soul and spirit, neither of the last two parts we can see with our body's eyes or touch with our hands. We are left to perceive their reality by other means. They are, however, no less real.

In fact, Christians believe that we are the only beings on earth that have a spiritual nature, which explains our ability to perceive and know God. It may help us to theorize that our spirits actually take part in, or draw their nature from, the *spiritual universe,* as we might call it. Our expectation of going to heaven is of our spirits' being released from their anchor in the universe with which our bodies are familiar, to exist fully in the spiritual universe instead.

Finite Existence

To say that heaven is a spiritual place, however, is not to suggest in any way that going there means the loss of bodily existence. Refer again to 1Co 15:4, where Paul was very precise and particular in talking about bodily existence in the spiritual realm. He seemed intent on disabusing us of any idea that when we die we are permanently disembodied.

Quite to the contrary, human existence is defined, at least in part, by bodily existence. Unlike God, who *is* spirit, we human beings are body and spirit. God is everywhere; we are in one place only. God exists in all times; we exist at one point in time only. God sees everything all at once; we see only what is around us with the bodies we have.

The best word to describe our existence both here and in the spiritual realm is *finite*. God is infinite; we are finite. The term means bounded in magnitude or spatial or temporal extent. While we expect, and have been promised, that eternal life grants us a never-ending life, our existence in heaven will still be finite in the sense that we will still occupy bodies that delimit us. We were not meant to be everywhere at all times. We were meant to be in one place at a time. That's simply how God created us.

We should therefore conclude, from the scriptures we have looked at so far, that heaven is a place just as real and tangible in its own sphere as we perceive our world here to be, and that our lives in heaven will be characterized by similar experiences of each other, of things, of movement, and of sight.

A Specific Place

Not only is heaven a spiritual place, but it is a specific place. Everywhere the Bible mentions heaven, it implies a specific location, not a general state. Especially in the accounts that dot the Old and New Testaments where people see heaven, see angels, see the throne of God, are taken up into heaven (2Ki 2:11), see Moses and Elijah in heaven (Lk 9:30), see Jesus at the right hand of God (Act 7:55), or are invited to come up to heaven (Rev 4:1), every indication is that heaven is a specific place. Its specificity is a corollary of its being a real and tangible place in its own realm.

Some other religions anticipate a general, incorporeal state of life after this one. To some people, apparently, this expectation is ideal. In their view, it represents a graduation from this physical universe into a superior state of mere consciousness, devoid of tactile experience, as one would have in a specific place. Sometimes people who don't commit themselves to any particular religion at all will philosophize that "heaven is a state of mind."

The Bible knows nothing of this sort of heaven. The heaven of the Bible is a specific place, the *location* of spiritual entities such as saints and angels. At least in the sense that he exhibits and reveals himself specially in heaven, God is there, too, though he exists everywhere else as well.

Naturally this specificity and reality of heaven invite the question of where heaven is. We have already touched on the possibility that heaven, a place created in the beginning, may be another universe unto itself. Even if the nature of heaven is something more sublime than another universe, we are still left wondering about where it might exist.

Beyond

We have already noted that the ancient Hebrew concept of there being three heavens placed God's dwelling in the third such heaven. The Hebrews had no developed cosmology beyond that, certainly none based on later discoveries of the truly spherical nature of the earth, the revolving of the earth around our sun, the sun's being one of billions of stars in the Milky Way galaxy, and our galaxy's being only one of billions of other galaxies in our universe. To the ancients, the third heaven was simply beyond the second heaven where the moon and stars are. They had no idea how far there was to go beyond the moon and a few stars!

What is relevant about the placement of the third heaven past the moon and stars is that it was perceived to be *beyond* what we can see with our eyes. That essential truth is what we should take from this limited cosmology.

Its being *beyond* us is an affirmation about its lack of intersection with our realm, at least on any regular basis. The exceptions to this fact serve only to accentuate its truth. For instance, when Jesus was baptized by John, Mat 3:16 says that "at that moment heaven was opened, and he saw the Spirit of God descending like a dove and lighting on him." In that account, "open" suggests a doorway, as if heaven were near, next, or even concurrent with our own place of existence. However, heaven had to be "opened," and clearly the only one who could open a portal for heaven and earth to intersect was God. For that brief moment, however, John the man saw the heaven from which Jesus had come by way of incarnation.

Another event we might call an intersection of heaven with this earth took place in Gen 22:11 where "the angel of the LORD called to [Abraham] out of heaven." There, only a voice penetrated from heaven to earth, at a key moment in the history of divine revelation. After Abraham looked where he was directed, there was no more voice. The brief portal was closed. Heaven remained *beyond*.

Apart

The Hebrews, like virtually everyone else in the ancient

world and the present one, conceived of heaven as above us. We point up when we talk of going to heaven. We point down when we speak of hell.

If we think about it in practical terms, it would be difficult to imagine our developing terminology for spiritual subjects in any other way. "Up" is universally associated with positive things just as "down" is with negative ones.

- Up is where light is, enabling us to see and know the world.
- Up is where we often aspire to be, to fly like the birds.
- Up is where the mountain peaks are, from which we can behold the beauty of the world more fully.
- Down is ground, difficult to penetrate and stifling to live below.
- Down is at first cool, shielded from the sun, but then increasingly hot towards the core of the earth, out of which volcanos arise.
- Down is where people are buried and rot, where death is.

However, the biblical association of heaven's location with a general, upward direction is merely a convenience. The problem with trying to fix heaven as being up is that up changes constantly. Twelve hours from the time you read these words, up will be down, since the earth rotates once every twenty-four hours. What is up right now will also be $180°$ on the opposite side of the universe from where you might be pointing at this moment.

The terminology of up for heaven (and down for hell) is a convenient shorthand for a longer discussion that the ancients might have had, and that we are having, to communicate the idea that heaven is *apart* from us. It is beyond our common, everyday reach. At some point, we will encounter it, but while we are alive, it is normally apart, or inaccessible to us.

Other

If the point of saying that heaven is up is to say that it is not on the earth, that idea, too, is probably ultimately in error. The Bible's description of heaven as a spiritual place means that it has no location in our physical world *at all.* Even if you decide not to incorporate theories of modern physics into your concept of heaven, you are still left with the biblical insistence that heaven cannot be reached by towers of Babel or huge catapults or any other means available to us in this world. It is *other,* just as God himself is *other.* Its nature and its location are both of some *other* kind.

We need to remind ourselves every time we read the word "up" in reference to heaven, such as in Rev 4:1-2, or in the ascension of Jesus in Act 1:10, that it is the common, universal use of this shorthand for locating what cannot be located by us. Undoubtedly, what the disciples saw when they saw Jesus ascend was his going up—what else were they going to see? Was God going to show them Jesus sinking down into, and merging with, the earth? Was Jesus going to shrink into a dot right before them and disappear? We are left with the inevitable conclusion that in myriad ways God accommodates our need to make sense of the things we perceive. "Up" is simply the best way for him to display what is happening on a far more sublime level than merely changing location from one place on the y-axis to another one above it.

Take, for instance, God's inspiration of Bible writers to speak of his face (Gen 33:10), his arm (Job 40:9), his hand (Ecc 9:1), or his back (Exo 33:23). These, too, are convenient terms in a sort of divine shorthand to speak of God's actions or attitudes. Other, straightforward teachings that do not rely on any metaphor or symbolism make it clear to us that God doesn't have form like we do. "God is spirit, and they that worship him must worship him in spirit and in truth" (Joh 4:24). We do not usually allow ourselves to think of God as some giant version of a human being; we must also insist on heaven's description as "up" as meaning that it is simply *other:* it is on another, entirely different, plane of existence.

Stewart Simms, Jr., for thirty years the pastor of Beech Haven Baptist Church in Athens, Georgia, wrote in his newsletter column one Christmas:

> This time of the year reminds us that One has traveled from beyond the stars to man. Jesus Christ, God in human flesh, left His unique place with the Father in heaven to come to us where we live... Heaven is pictured as being "above" in order to symbolize its complete 'differentness' from anything we can conceive. Who knows? It may be beyond the stars. It may be far away. Or, if Einstein was right and the universe wraps around itself, heaven may be very close. While we are unsure exactly where heaven is, we can be very sure that it is where God is, and we can be sure how to get there. Jesus said, "I am the Way, the Truth and the Life; no man cometh to the Father but by me."

If we were able to discover exactly where heaven is and what its metaphysical structure or composition is, we would have acquired information of much, much lesser importance than we really need. Of far greater worth to us should be our knowing who is in heaven, who is *going* to heaven, and how to be included among those people. Look now at what the Bible teaches about this vital question.

3
Who is in Heaven?

The world's main religions differ on the nature and location of heaven. Sects within these religions have an even wider variety in their conceptions. Not surprisingly, people of differing religious beliefs also have different opinions of who resides in heaven at any given time, past, present or future. Our study is concerned not with a comparison of world religions or even of Christian sects, but with a direct investigation of what the Bible says about the question of who is in heaven.

God the Father

In the New Testament there are twenty-one references to God the Father's being in heaven. The Old Testament speaks in numerous places of God (usually identifiable with God the Father) as being in heaven, speaking from heaven, acting out of heaven, etc. The first and most obvious fact about heaven's occupancy is that God the Father is there.

In Deu 26:15, Moses wrote, "Look down from heaven, your holy dwelling place, and bless your people Israel and the land you have given us." In a sense—as long as we realize it is a limited sense as discussed in the previous chapter—heaven is God's home. In some special way, he makes himself known in his creation by a glorious and powerful presence in heaven.

The word used for "dwelling place" in this verse is used elsewhere to describe people's homes. Other passages where heaven is described as God (the Father's) dwelling place include 1Ki 8:30,39,43, 2Ch 6:21 and 30:27. (The tabernacle, temple, and the city of Zion are also spoken of as places where God dwells, but in another sense.)

In 1Ki 8:30 Solomon, when dedicating the temple, said, "Hear the supplication of your servant and of your people Israel when they pray toward this place. Hear from heaven, your dwelling place, and when you hear, forgive." What can be derived immediately from this inspired verse is that God, in heaven and from heaven, can hear and know what is said and done here. Nothing about his being in heaven limits the fact that he is also omnipresent and omniscient.

Scripture teaches that God is everywhere at once. The Psalmist wrote in 139:7-12, "Where can I go from your spirit? or whither shall I flee from thy presence? If I ascend up into heaven, thou art there: if I make my bed in hell, behold, thou art there." God does not follow us around: he is already everywhere we could ever be. This is the supernatural attribute of omnipresence.

Yet God has given himself a locale, a specific place of his making, where his glory is exhibited in a special way, apparently for the benefit of all created beings. This place is heaven. We would easily be able to infer that in the absence of anything else—any created thing, including angels and people—God didn't need a heaven. He is sufficient unto himself. He created heaven to go along with the rest of his creation, as a demonstration of his majesty.

Far from being an exercise in vanity, God's creation of a majestic and glorious place for his special dwelling is reflected in our own sense that dignified and important institutions and entities deserve impressive buildings and monuments. Does any of us fault the United States of America for building a magnificent Capitol or a stately White House? Regardless of the individual people who may bring honor or dishonor to those places, they are symbols of the country that was brought into existence as a bastion of freedom and a nation of justice. They represent an ideal for which we strive.

God's heaven is no doubt a glorious place, and his creation of it as a visible (in the heavenly realm) outworking of his own glory is absolutely fitting for the God of the Universe, who is perfect and beyond compare.

God's Throne Room

Not only is God the Father present in heaven, he uses it as his throne room. The Psalmist wrote in 123:1, "I lift up my eyes to you, to you whose throne is in heaven." This specific statement says that God reigns from heaven. It is a place of glory as the throne room of God.

Joining that verse is 1Ki 22:19, where the prophet Michaiah said, "Hear thou therefore the word of the LORD: I saw the LORD sitting on his throne, and all the host of heaven standing by him on his right hand and on his left." We must consider the idea that in the realms of heaven, where as we will see, angels and people also dwell, God conducts a certain pageantry associated with the larger rule of his creation. We can infer, from what we know of the nature of God and the needs of his creation, that he does this for our benefit, that we might be properly awed by the sovereign control he exercises over all he has made.

Psa 11:4 likewise states that "the LORD'S throne is in heaven: his eyes behold, his eyelids try, the children of men." Psalm 45:6 speaks of God's throne being forever and ever, and references "the scepter of thy kingdom."

It is probably wise for us to apply to the throne and the scepter in God's heaven the same principle we apply to God's hand, arm, and face, and to the concept of heaven's being upward in direction. Whether or not God actually sits on a throne in heaven or holds a scepter visible "up" there, these words identify the symbols of rule commonly employed in earthly kingdoms. In describing God's rule, they communicate his perfected activity of the same kind. He sits in judgment and sovereignty: thus he has a throne. He rules with glorious justice: thus he has a scepter.

Expanding the symbolism a bit, Isaiah wrote that "The heaven is my throne and the earth is my footstool" (Isa 66:1). Isaiah's terminology suggests that God doesn't merely have a throne in heaven, but that all heaven is the place from which he rules. Jesus himself said in Mat 5:34 that heaven "is God's throne." Clearly the throne of God is a symbol, even if it exists as a heavenly object (which certain verses in Revelation clearly indicate). The impact of the Bible's total message about God's throne in heaven is that from heaven God rules the earth and his entire universe with perfect justice and limitless power and glory.

A few years ago, Harritte Thompson, a woman who had served notably and honorably at the Central Intelligence Agency was honored with the creation of a chair there, the Chair for Resource Management at the George Bush Center for Intelligence. There is no actual such chair with a seat and four legs in any building where anyone sits. The chair is an idea, a principle, and a position. Someone will occupy a place of responsibility commensurate with the groundbreaking work of Harritte Thompson in the area of resource management.

Curiously, however, a few days after Thompson, by then retired, arrived home again, a shipping crate appeared on her front porch. Inside was an ornate black chair decorated in gold bands, featuring the seal of the CIA on its back and an inscription identifying the specific honor that had been bestowed on Thompson. Thus, her chair was both an idea and an object. The object represented the greater concept of her work and her legacy.

God's throne in heaven is of the same kind. Visions of heaven may establish that an actual throne exists there and that God reveals himself gloriously at or upon it. However, God does not depend upon a chair for his authority. He ruled sovereignly before there was anything. Now that there is a creation, he includes visual aids, we might say, for the benefit of his creatures, to symbolize his majesty and power and to inspire awe in his presence.

God the Son

Just as God the Father is in heaven, God the Son, Jesus Christ, is in heaven. Many references in the Bible describe the position of Jesus as the risen and glorified Son in a prominent place in heaven. Commenting on all of them would be overkill to make the point, but here are some of the main ones:

> • Act 7:55 - "But he, being full of the Holy Ghost, looked up stedfastly into heaven, and saw the glory of God, and Jesus standing on the right hand of God" - The deacon Stephen was stoned for his powerful preaching, and Christ honored him with a vision of himself in heaven, with God, where Stephen would momentarily be.
> • Joh 13:1 - "Now before the feast of the passover, when Jesus knew that his hour was come that he should depart out of this world unto the Father..." - Although the word "heaven" is not actually in this verse, we have already established that the Father is in heaven. Consequently, Jesus' return to the Father necessarily means he was

shortly to be in heaven himself.

• Act 1:11 - "Ye men of Galilee, why stand ye gazing up into heaven? this same Jesus, which is taken up from you into heaven, shall so come in like manner as ye have seen him go into heaven." - The ascension of Jesus was his transmission from this realm into the spiritual realm and heaven. His second coming will be from heaven to earth again, though in conquering glory rather than obscure birth.

• Rev 5:6 - "And I beheld, and, lo, in the midst of the throne and of the four beasts, and in the midst of the elders, stood a Lamb as it had been slain, having seven horns and seven eyes, which are the seven Spirits of God sent forth into all the earth." - John's revelation included a highly symbolic representation of Christ in heaven. The Lamb is one of his favorite words for Jesus, and in this particular appearance John saw a lamb instead of a human figure. No doubt the choice of how John would perceive Jesus at that moment was Christ's. The essential point for our study is that Jesus Christ is in heaven.

Not only is Jesus Christ, the ascended Savior, in heaven with the Father, but New Testament writers position him variously with respect to the throne:

• Mat 19:28 - "...in the regeneration when the Son of man will sit in the throne of his glory"
• Mat 25:31 - "When the Son of man will come in his glory, and all the holy angels with him, then will he sit upon the throne of his glory"
• Heb 1:8 - "But unto the Son he saith, Thy throne, O God, is forever and ever: a scepter of righteousness is the scepter of thy kingdom."

- Heb 8:1 - "We have such an high priest, who is set on the right hand of the throne of the Majesty in the heavens"
- Heb 12:2 - "Looking unto Jesus the author and finisher of our faith; who for the joy that was set before him endured the cross, despising the shame, and is set down at the right hand of the throne of God."
- Rev 3:21 - "To him that overcometh will I grant to sit with me in my throne, even as I also overcame, and am set down with my Father in his throne."

Notice that the first four verses plainly say that the throne is that of the Son of God, Jesus Christ. The fifth and sixth say that Christ is now *at the right hand* of the throne of God (the Father). If we insist on a rigid, wooden interpretation of these words, we have a conflict. Is it the Father's throne or the Son's? Fortunately, scripture itself leads us to relax our interpretation, as it explains to us in the final scripture, Rev 3:21, that Jesus occupies the throne with his Father.

We needn't try to construct this throne in our imaginations as a "two seater," solely for the purpose of imagining what people who have glimpsed heaven have seen. The imagery of the Bible is not meant for this purpose. Furthermore, since the Bible presents God as triune, existing as one God in three persons, it shouldn't surprise us that the throne of God may in one place be spoken of as that of the Father and in another place as the throne of the Son. Rev 5:6 also mentions that incorporated in the imagery of Christ on the throne was the representation of God the Spirit. The biblical authors either employed what imagery suited their purpose in proclaiming spiritual truths, or they recorded the imagery they may have seen in visions, which makes God himself the one who chose the images to project or reveal to them.

The point is that Jesus Christ, the God-Man, the incarnate Son who lived, died and rose again, went from earth to heaven and resides there now. He did as he prayed in Joh 17: he reclaimed the glory he had with the Father "before the world was."

There and Here

As a sidebar, we should note that while Jesus the glorified, incarnate Savior, is in heaven, his presence is made known in this world in each of his followers and in the church.

Jesus taught his disciples in Joh 15:4 that "I will remain in you," and in 16:13-15, "the Spirit of truth comes [to] take what is mine and make it known to you." Jesus, who abides in heaven, is known through the Spirit of God in believers. The Christian's experience of Jesus Christ is mediated by the Holy Spirit, who is after all the Spirit of Christ (Rom 8:9, 1Pe 1:11). Since God the Spirit has all the attributes of the triune God, he is omnipresent—not limited to either heaven or earth.

Angels

God's creation in the beginning generated everything that exists, including the angels. Angels are not divine beings and they do not have God's attribute of eternal existence. At some point, angels came into being. Heaven is the place or realm where angels may be said to have their primary dwelling.

> • Gen 28:12 - "And he dreamed, and behold a ladder set up on the earth, and the top of it reached to heaven: and behold the angels of God ascending and descending on it." In Jacob's famous vision of the ladder, he saw angels both going into and also coming out of heaven. Simply from the standpoint of other statements in scripture that angels

operate in the earth, we can easily see that heaven is their base of operations, from which they are sent on divinely appointed missions having to do with human beings and other things. The word "angel" means "messenger." Sometimes their messages are words; other times, their messages are distinctly more powerful, and occasionally destructive, actions.

• Mar 12:25 - "For when they shall rise from the dead, they neither marry, nor are given in marriage; but are as the angels which are in heaven." This comment about the nature of angels happens to mention also that they are in heaven. The heavenly or spiritual realm is their home territory, so to speak.

• Eze 1 - Ezekiel's vision of a wheel within a wheel and the four creatures associated with it is tied to the identity of cherubim in Eze 10:2. Closely associated with that vision is a similar record from Isa 6:2ff where the prophet saw angelic creatures he called seraphim. The cherubim and seraphim are apparently a small number of specialized angels whose dwelling is exclusively in heaven and who seem to incorporate and invoke the constant worship of God and the recognition of his awesome presence.

• Rev 4:6 - "...and round about the throne, were four beasts full of eyes before and behind." - John's vision of the throne of God included a description of creatures so wildly magnificent and awesome that he could only stab at words to represent them. They appear to have been the angels either Ezekiel or Isaiah recounted seeing.

Most of us are not surprised that God the Father, God the Son, and the angels, are in heaven. What we are interested in knowing at a very personal level is about the presence of human beings in heaven, both now and prospectively.

Old Testament Saints

"Old Testament saints" is a generally recognized term referring to those persons connected to the Jewish faith prior to the coming of Christ who were not only part of the nation but were also people of faith in God whose hearts were right with him. Certainly they would include Moses, David, the prophets, and other prominent figures who were revered as leaders in God's way; however, they would also include myriad people who constituted the nation and who loved God genuinely. They might be described as those who followed the prophetic assessment of righteous living:

> He hath shewed thee, O man, what is good; and what doth the Lord require of thee, but to do justly, and to love mercy, and to walk humbly with thy God? Mic 6:8

Paul later described the Old Testament saint when he said:

> For they are not all Israel, which are of Israel: Neither, because they are the seed of Abraham, are they all children: but, In Isaac shall thy seed be called. That is, They which are the children of the flesh, these are not the children of God: but the children of the promise are counted for the seed. - Rom 9:6-8

Paul had earlier written in Rom 3:1-10 that the children of promise are those who have faith in God's saving work, which ultimately was Jesus Christ. So the Old Testament saint was not simply any Jew, but those Jews who grasped the promises of God revealed to the Jews and trusted God for his righteousness to be worked in their lives as they walked humbly and obediently with him.

Differing Views

Religious groups differ on the question of whether or not Old Testament saints are currently in heaven. Some Christian groups divide the possible abode of Old Testament saints into all sorts of compartmental destinations. Hades is sometimes paired with Paradise, Sheol made into a general destination not quite heaven, or Abraham's Bosom becomes a specialized area of the afterlife.

One of the major Old Testament references to Old Testament saints and their destination upon death is 2Ki 2:1:

> When the LORD was about to take Elijah up to heaven in a whirlwind, Elijah and Elisha were on their way from Gilgal. ...As they were walking along and talking together, suddenly a chariot of fire and horses of fire appeared and separated the two of them, and Elijah went up to heaven in a whirlwind.

Some groups insist that Elijah did *not* go to heaven, that his experience of being taken up into heaven was rather "into the heavens." However, all the major translations have "heaven" in both 2Ki 2:1 and 11.

Some teachers will point to Jesus' statement in Joh 3:13 that "no man hath ascended up to heaven but he that came down from heaven, even the Son of Man which is in heaven." They insist that this means that before Jesus came, died, rose and ascended, nobody but God and angels was ever in heaven. The problem with this interpretation is that it is not consistent with other scriptural statements and clear implications. 2Ki 2:1,11 say that Elijah went to heaven. We have already noted that Paul's account in 2Co 12:2-4 equates the third heaven—God's abode—with Paradise. Those who hold the view that no person before Christ went to heaven simply suggest that Paradise itself was lifted out of where it was (which would have been *sheol* or *hades* in their view) and transferred to heaven once Jesus ascended. This kind of rationalization is unnecessary and artificial.

When Jesus said that no one had ascended into heaven, he was contrasting the role of previous great leaders, such as Moses (whom he then mentions), who lived wonderful lives and did great things but who died and *did not rise again* and did not then *ascend to heaven triumphantly.* Even Elijah's going up into heaven in a chariot of fire was not an ascension in the same way as that of Jesus—and no one ever suggests that it was. In Joh 3:13, Jesus was talking about his messianic role; no one shared that role. In *no one else* was salvation to be found but the one who was incarnated, who conquered death, and then *ascended.*

While some Christians hold that Old Testament saints did not go to heaven when they died *before Christ,* they did go into heaven when Christ ascended. The bottom line for this position is that now, in the church age, the Old Testament saints are in heaven.

Contrasting with Christian views almost 180° is the Jehovah's Witness view that only 144,000 people will be in heaven, irrespective of their relationship to the Old or New Testaments. This interpretation is so out of phase with the New Testament, and so out of harmony with the tested and verified teachings of orthodox Christianity, that it simply must not be considered here.

New Testament Witness

Another New Testament passage reflecting the presence of Old Testament saints in heaven is Luk 9:29-32:

And as he prayed, the fashion of his countenance was

altered, and his raiment was white and glistering. And, behold, there talked with him two men, which were Moses and Elias: Who appeared in glory, and spake of his decease which he should accomplish at Jerusalem. But Peter and they that were with him were heavy with sleep: and when they were awake, they saw his glory, and the two men that stood with him.

We should carefully note that the word "heaven" is not used in this account. However, the place where Jesus, Moses, and Elias (Elijah) met does not comport with any implications left by either the Old Testament term *sheol* or the New Testament word *hades*. Rather, we have a description of brilliant and glorious surroundings. If we were to assign a name to the place the disciples saw, it would almost certainly have to be heaven.

During this moment that has come to be called the Transfiguration, Jesus assumed his spiritual glory, and the realm of heaven broke open into earth and intermingled with it for a few moments on a mountainside. Moses and Elijah were there. The obvious conclusion is that Old Testament saints must be in heaven.

Without our taking the time to work through all the positions and arguments made by this or that Christian sect or teacher, it is simply a fact that too much quibbling and artificial differentiating is done in trying to determine what is probably a fact more simply discerned from the plain images of scripture.

The Bible contains a variety of terms for death and afterlife, graduating in both sentiment and scope from the earliest of times to the rather complete picture of the book of Revelation.

Abraham's Bosom was a term Jesus used in Luk 16:22 for

the abode of the godly after death. While it doesn't appear as such a term in the Old Testament, it predated Jesus in Jewish history. Its value lies principally in the sentimental connection of Jews with their ultimate parent in flesh and faith, Abraham. It is equivalent to the Old Testament way of saying that one slept with his fathers. When David said of his deceased baby, "I shall go to him, but he shall not return to me" (2Sa 12:23), he was speaking of this familial destination.

Another term generally sufficed in the Old Testament for the destination of *all* people when we die. The word is *sheol,* meaning the grave or the unseen state (Deu 32:22, 2Sa 22:6, Job 11:8, 26:6, Psa 9:17, 16:10, 18:5, 55:15, 86:13, 116:3, 139:8, Pro 5:5, 7:27, 9:18, 15:11,24, 23:14, 27:20, Isa 5:14, 14:9,15, 28:15,18, 57:9, Eze 31:16, 32:21,27, Amo 9:2, Joh 2:2, Hab 2:5). Older versions including the King James do not transliterate *sheol* into an Anglicized word in these verses but merely render it "hell." Context shows us in most cases that the word doesn't mean what we mean today when we say "hell." *Sheol* deserved its own transliteration. Sheol as a place was generally undifferentiated between its character as a destination for the righteous or the wicked.

In other Old Testament verses, *sheol* is translated "grave" (Gen 37:35, 42:38, 1Sa 2:6, Job 21:13, Psa 89:48, etc.). The overall sense derived from the Old Testament phraseology is that what lay beyond death was a vast unknown. To the faithful Jew, his sense was that the righteous were comforted and the wicked were punished there, but the common grief and mystery surrounding the destiny of the departed, whether righteous or wicked, was often summarized by the generalization that they simply joined the congregation of the dead.

Revelation of *all* spiritual truth was gradual and progressive. We should not be surprised that God's people came to a deeper understanding of eternal destinations over the millennia.

In the New Testament, the Greek word *hades* had a similar range of meanings to the Hebrew *sheol*. It was downward (Mat 11:23) and it was seen as having a prison (1Pe 3:19, in some interpretations). Yet even those who locate Abraham's bosom in it (Luk 16:23) acknowledge that in the realm of the dead there was a division between the righteous and the wicked. Jesus called it "a great gulf fixed" (Luk 16:26).

The bottom line is that certainly now, in the church age, the time after the coming of Jesus Christ, Old Testament saints are not relegated to some vague realm of the dead but are residents of heaven, where God and Christ and the angels live. The totality of the picture given us in the Bible asserts that this is so.

The Born-Again in Christ

Of greatest importance to the Christian living now is to know with assurance that he or she will be in heaven upon taking his last breath on earth. The overwhelming teaching of the Bible is that this is so. The believer's confidence is well founded that his salvation in Christ includes the promise that death leads immediately to being in the presence of his Savior.

It is surprising there can be any difference of opinion by groups that generally hold the Bible as an authority, but such differences do exist.

Some groups say departed believers are not in heaven yet, but instead await resurrection in some state, whether in a condition of "soul-sleep" or conscious on some plane.

Many of our Catholic friends believe the departed may not yet go to heaven because they go instead to purgatory.

Purgatory, defined in the Catechism of the Roman Catholic Church, is a place of "purification, so as to achieve the holiness necessary to enter the joy of heaven." Catholics regard purgatory as a sort of penal way station on the way to heaven. It is largely the creation of popes and bishops around the sixth century A.D., notably Pope Gregory the Great, having emerged during the period when the Bishop of Rome was established as the authority over all others. This was the period during which Catholicism developed the two-pronged authorities of scripture and the teachings of the Church. Purgatory as a place beyond this life is not taught in the Bible, only in the doctrines of the Catholic church.

Our study is without apology limited to the teachings of the Bible. The Bible is comfortingly clear about the destination of the Christian upon death. The believer, a born-again person in Christ, goes to heaven when he dies.

There are twenty-three references in the New Testament to believers going to or being in heaven. In most of these instances, the scripture implies directly that heavenly existence begins immediately after this life ends.

The main references make our case strongly:

- Luk 23:43 - "And he said unto Jesus, Lord, remember me when thou comest into thy kingdom. And Jesus said unto him, Verily I say unto thee, To day shalt thou be with me in paradise." This conversation is what courts would call "best evidence." Jesus himself, the King of the Kingdom of Heaven, gave a promise to the penitent thief on the cross that he would be with him in paradise that very day, within a short time, in fact, as they both died. Having located paradise in heaven and probably as synonymous with it, we can be very certain that Jesus meant that both he and the penitent thief were headed for the heaven of

the Father, the angels, and saints of the past.
• Joh 14:1-4 - "Let not your heart be troubled: ye believe in God, believe also in me. In my Father's house are many mansions: if it were not so, I would have told you. I go to prepare a place for you. And if I go and prepare a place for you, I will come again, and receive you unto myself; that where I am, there ye may be also. And whither I go ye know, and the way ye know." Again, Jesus directly addressed his disciples about heaven, "my Father's house." He spoke of "mansions," something we will look at further in the study, and told them he was going there to prepare a place for them. We cannot go much further than his words in particularly describing these dwelling places without engaging in pure speculation. What is doubtless is that Jesus was assuring his followers a place in heaven, to be ushered there by Christ himself.
• 2Co 5:6-8 - "Therefore we are always confident, knowing that, whilst we are at home in the body, we are absent from the Lord: (For we walk by faith, not by sight:) We are confident, I say, and willing rather to be absent from the body, and to be present with the Lord." This passage from one of Paul's letters offered only two options for the location of the Christian: in the body, which is to be absent from the immediate presence of Jesus Christ the Lord; or absent from the body, which is to be in the immediate presence of the Lord. There is no other possibility, according to the very direct assessment of the Apostle. Once we cease to be in this world in spirit, we will be in the heavenly realm. The transition appears to be automatic and immediate.

True Home

Jesus' teachings and the explanations of them offered by

the apostles in the rest of the New Testament posit heaven as not just a destination, but rather the true home of the Christian. The testimony of Col 1:16 is that not just the Christian but all people were "created by him [Christ], and for him." Sin broke the relationship between people and God and brought about the necessity of salvation to regain a right standing with him. Many people will never be brought to salvation; Christians are those who have been given the grace of repentance and faith in Christ and placed back on the road to eternal life with their Creator. In that most fundamental sense, then, Christians are not at home in this world, especially since the world has come under the condemnation of sin.

God's plan is to redeem all creation (Rom 8:22-23) and to bring about a new heavens and earth (2Pe 3:13). Until that time, every person born, finding salvation in Christ, and moving through this life toward its tough conclusion in physical death, is in reality on a pilgrimage to his true home. As Taylor Cassel's 1902 hymn began: "I am a stranger here, within a foreign land; My home is far away, upon a golden strand."

Another old and traditional song plaintively describes how the Christian doesn't really belong in this world after coming to the saving knowledge of Christ:

> I'm just a poor wayfaring stranger
> A' traveling through this world of woe;
> Yet there's no sickness, toil or danger
> In that bright land to which I go.
> I'm going there to see my Father;
> I'm going there no more to roam;
> I'm just a' going over Jordan;
> I'm just a' going over home.

The point of such hymns—and there are numerous others with this theme—was not to suggest that the Christian should cut himself off from the needs of the world or the mission of Christ in this world, but that the believer should deal with the stresses, troubles, challenges, and opportunities of this life as one whose real goals are heavenly, not earthly. Further, the believer must recognize that his true fulfillment, true wealth, true reward and ultimate satisfaction are not to be found in the passing things of this world, but in the eternal things of his heavenly destination—his true home.

A survey of some of Jesus' and his apostles' teachings makes this point abundantly clear:

Our true treasure is in heaven. Mat 6:20 - "But lay up for yourselves treasures in heaven, where neither moth nor rust doth corrupt, and where thieves do not break through nor steal." Mat 19:21 - "Jesus said unto him, If thou wilt be perfect, go and sell that thou hast, and give to the poor, and thou shalt have treasure in heaven: and come and follow me." Mar 10:21 - "Then Jesus beholding him loved him, and said unto him, One thing thou lackest: go thy way, sell whatsoever thou hast, and give to the poor, and thou shalt have treasure in heaven: and come, take up the cross, and follow me."

It is notable that Jesus delivered the challenging maxim in his Sermon on the Mount largely to people who were poor and downtrodden—people who didn't have much if any treasure on earth. In the case where he promised treasure in heaven to a rich young man, the fellow went away sad precisely because of his wealth, which Jesus proposed that he part with entirely. In general, there is a sliding scale between the utterly dispossessed at one end and the fabulously wealthy on the other: the willingness, indeed the urgency, to see heaven as the place of our true treasure is very great on the part of the former and nearly nonexistent on the part of the latter. To be sure, some poor people insist on making the dream of worldly wealth their god, and some rich people do recognize that their true riches lie in the knowledge of Christ, but the exceptions tend to prove the rule.

The fact that Jesus spoke of our true treasure as being in heaven underscores the promise that the believer is certain to be taken to heaven upon death. If we were to forsake worldly wealth for heavenly treasure and then not receive it, not only would the promise of salvation have been untrustworthy, but our self-denial during even our brief lives on earth would have been for nothing.

Our reward is in heaven. Mat 5:12 - "Rejoice, and be exceeding glad: for great is your reward in heaven: for so persecuted they the prophets which were before you." Luk 6:23 - "Rejoice ye in that day, and leap for joy: for, behold, your reward is great in heaven: for in the like manner did their fathers unto the prophets."

The concept of heavenly reward is found several places in the New Testament and has prompted widely varying guesses as to what it might consist of. The scope of this study does not include an extensive digression into heavenly reward or rewards, but clearly Jesus promised that upon going to heaven, rewards would be given.

Rewards differ from treasure mostly in the reason for their receipt. The two verses cited have a context of persecution. Believers who resist the temptation to cave into the pressures of the world, who stand up to persecution and endure it, who are victorious in the witness of their lives and words in the face of opposition, will be rewarded. Treasures by contrast seem more connected to loving and sacrificial service, irrespective of any resistance or persecution encountered.

Again, the promise of reward in heaven underscores the

certainty the Christian has of his heavenly destination. The believer may rest assured that the cost of his discipleship, however high it might be, is not wasted, because he is guaranteed that when he passes from this life, he enters immediately into heaven where every injustice will be made up for.

Our citizenship is in heaven. Php 3:20 - "For our conversation is in heaven; from whence also we look for the Saviour, the Lord Jesus Christ." Paul's word here for "conversation" was *politeuma,* which meant the administration of civil affairs, or in the case of one person, *citizenship.* The Christian shares his true commonality with other Christians and he belongs in an atmosphere perfectly ruled by Jesus Christ. Even the best society in the world in the best of lands under the most beneficent of governments is greatly imperfect. Heaven will be peopled only by those perfected in Christ and will be governed—to the extent that it needs any government at all—by the perfect, triune God.

While the impoverished Christian may find it difficult to hold out his hope for heavenly treasure when the need of earthly things may be intense, most believers realize quickly that life in this world leaves a great deal to be desired in the way of justice, equality, and brotherly love. The promise of Christ is a heavenly realm where all these longings are fulfilled.

Our eternal possessions are in heaven. Heb 10:34 - "For ye had compassion of me in my bonds, and took joyfully the spoiling of your goods, knowing in yourselves that ye have in heaven a better and an enduring substance." 1Pe 1:4 - "To an inheritance incorruptible, and undefiled, and that fadeth not away, reserved in heaven for you." Paul's word "substance" indicated earthly possessions including money. Those who contributed sacrificially to Paul's ministry knew they would have permanent possessions in heaven.

Jim Elliot, a young missionary who was martyred while laboring among the Auca people of Ecuador in 1956, wrote in his diary: "He is no fool who gives what he cannot keep to gain that which he cannot lose." Seventeenth century Philip Henry said something very similar. The principle is here in Paul's teachings, who simply rephrased what Jesus himself taught.

A popular party game that goes by several names requires participants to bring unwrapped gifts which are then randomly redistributed. Going around a circle, each person then has the option of keeping what he has or taking another person's gift by "trading." Really good gifts are stolen often, and the last person in the circle has the advantage of the final swap. People must enjoy the game since it is played so often, but it encourages covetousness, even if only in fun. It also makes the point, however, that you may have something one moment and lose it the next. Our possessions in this world are fleeting at best.

The promise of permanent substance or possessions in heaven may prompt daydreaming as to what they might be, but the question is irrelevant. The crucial truth is that Christians will be people of permanent possessions in the place of permanent and eternal life.

Our hope is in heaven. Col 1:5 - "For the hope which is laid up for you in heaven, whereof ye heard before in the word of the truth of the gospel..." The force of this hope of which the Apostle spoke is salvation itself, or more specifically, the person of the Savior, Jesus Christ. Paul's salutation in 1Ti 1:1 referenced "Lord Jesus Christ, which is our hope." This hope is the summation of all we expect to inherit in Christ. First and foremost, our expectation is to see, know, and experience Jesus Christ himself.

The 1998 film *What Dreams May Come* tells the story of a man who dies in an accident and experiences heaven. As part of the plot, the viewer is shown families and friends in heaven who are wonderfully loving and social, and vistas in heaven that are enchantingly beautiful. What is notably absent, however, is the personal presence of God, particularly in the person of Jesus Christ. The film is not strictly based on an orthodox Christian set of beliefs.

What will make heaven most glorious for the Christian is not how beautiful every*thing* there may be, but in the inexpressible joy of seeing and knowing Jesus Christ regularly and continually. He is the sole reason any person will be in heaven in the first place. While on earth we sometimes tire of the company of even our best of friends, the Christian will never tire of being in the presence of God his Savior.

Our names are written in heaven. Luk 10:20 - "Notwithstanding in this rejoice not, that the spirits are subject unto you; but rather rejoice, because your names are written in heaven." Heb 12:23 - "To the general assembly and church of the firstborn, which are written in heaven, and to God the Judge of all, and to the spirits of just men made perfect..." Rev 21:27 - "And there shall in no wise enter into it any thing that defileth, neither whatsoever worketh abomination, or maketh a lie: but they which are written in the Lamb's book of life." The scripture's guarantee of the Christian's going to heaven when he dies is underscored by the emphatic statement in several places that his name is written in heaven. Our arrival is expected.

A person who arrives at a conference only to find that his name is not on the list of registered persons experiences distress and perhaps confusion. Perhaps he misunderstood the requirements of registration, or failed to send a form, or forgot to pay a fee. Occasionally someone has this experience but then discovers that his name was spelled wrong or the registrar overlooked his name on the list.

Human beings may misunderstand the requirements of going to heaven, but heaven's registrar never makes mistakes. A person may miss his opportunity to go to heaven by failing to come through Jesus Christ, but everyone who has repented of sin and received the Christ as Saving Lord has his name clearly and securely written in heaven.

Whether or not there is an actual list in heaven, a name on a stone, a plaque on a mansion, or any other inscription with any particular Christian's name, the point of the scripture's promise is that God guarantees the believer's entrance into heaven because he has personal knowledge of that Christian. We can be relatively certain there are no pearly gates where constantly St. Peter sits, looking up names of people lined up for entry, as jokes about heaven often begin. Revelation 21:21 does mention twelve gates around the New Jerusalem that "were pearls," but our comic book depiction of things trivializes the likely reality.

Neither will anyone need to look up the name of a Christian who, freed from his damaged earthly body, appears in the heavenly realm for entry into his eternal abode. God knows every one of us by name. This is the point of the expression that Christians' names are written in heaven: our admission is guaranteed.

The population of heaven, then, is made up of our triune God, the angels he created, Old Testament saints, and New Testament saints—persons born again through faith in Jesus Christ. Now we look back into the pages of the Bible for the answer to a question that perennially rises in the minds of parents everywhere. What about young children and infants? If they die before they are old enough to understand any of the Bible's truths about sin and salvation, what happens to them?

A story making the news in 2014 featured parents who found out during the mother's pregnancy that her little girl had developed a life-ending brain abnormality that would almost certainly result in her death *in utero*. If she survived birth, she would live only a short while. The parents accepted the reality and planned to document photographically the birth and what moments they might have with their daughter before she died. She was, in fact, born alive and she lived about ten minutes. During that time they loved on her, bonded with her and celebrated her brief presence in this world. Then the little girl died peacefully.

Is there any way we can conceive of the notion that this helpless little girl was loved and celebrated in this world for ten minutes and then departed to be separated from God forever in a place prepared for the devil and his angels? Or should we rather say that it should seem morally self-evident that infants are forever in the hands of God and go to be with him?

Unaccountable Children

It is this writer's conviction that children who die, not having reached what most evangelical Christians call "the age of accountability," will be included in heaven. A defense of that position does not consist of merely a moral and emotional argument that any other position would seem heartless and entirely inconsistent with the justice of God. In fact, a defense can be undertaken using some familiar verses of scripture.

First, 1Co 7:14 says, "The unbelieving husband is sanctified through his wife, and the unbelieving wife has been sanctified through her believing husband. Otherwise your children would be unclean, but as it is, they are holy" (NIV). Some interpreters would apply the term "Christian" somewhat loosely to young children of believers, while others would employ some circumlocution, preferring to save "Christian" for those meeting the standard of having personally responded to the gospel in faith.

Probably Paul's statement was not meant as a blanket guarantee that any child who had at least one Christian parent was headed to heaven. Note that Paul didn't specify whether or not the children he had in mind were five years old or fifteen. What Paul probably meant was that these children had the advantage of Christian upbringing and leading toward faith.

However, the verse makes many evangelical Christians uncomfortable, in that it raises the issue of their children's spiritual estate prior to an age at which they might in any conceivable fashion be thought to understand either sin or salvation. By one route or another, most Christians, especially those who are parents, come to believe that while their very young children may not technically be saved, they are nevertheless safe.

Is this viewpoint supported by the New Testament? Again, this writer believes it is.

When we talk about the age of accountability, it's our way of dealing with something we believe is scriptural in principle but isn't discussed in the Bible in an A-B-C fashion. It is a concept gathered from the general picture of children in the Bible, what we know of God and his justice, and what we know of Jesus in his redemption.

Mar 10:14 records Jesus as having said, "Suffer the little children to come unto me, and forbid them not: for of such is the kingdom of God." In part, Jesus was pointing to something about children that all people need to emulate, namely the ease with which children trust and love. However, Jesus also seemed to be talking about their innocence, their absence, as yet, of corruption. I believe Jesus was implying that children, so long as they are too young to make a moral choice, to choose sin for themselves, are under the eternal protection of God.

Jesus' statement about children and heaven may be further elucidated by something Paul said about his own experience.

In Romans 7:9 Paul said, "Once I was alive apart from law; but when the commandment came, sin sprang to life and I died" (NIV). Was Paul talking about childhood or his pre-Christian life, as an adult? Scholars are divided, but substantial numbers of competent Bible scholars believe Paul meant that there is a condition of life before being old enough to understand sin, in which the young child is secure for eternity with God. When the first actual, responsible sin is committed, however, that innocence and its protection end.

Some years ago the author performed the wedding of a couple in Christian ministry and then watched as they built their family. Their first son was a typical boy, boisterous and active. Years later, the young father recounted to me a particular day, sometime in his son's eighth year, when he was given an instruction by his mother. The boy looked up with an unusually independent expression and blurted out, "No!" The father said he was struck dramatically and conclusively with the import of that moment. He said, "I will never forget it. I believed I had watched the very first knowing decision to sin. It was as if the light of the grace of God left his little face and a dark cloud of sin came over him. I believe that day he became responsible for sin and started needing a Savior."

Whether such anecdotal evidence proves anything or not, it fits with what the Scripture says about the children Jesus saw as illustrative of the citizenry of heaven, and it seems to be in harmony with what Paul said about the moment "the commandment came, sin sprang to life, and I died."

Compare these scriptures and conclusions, then, with Romans 2:12-15:

> For as many as have sinned without law shall also perish without law: and as many as have sinned in the law shall be judged by the law; (For not the hearers of the law are just before God, but the doers of the law shall be justified.) For when the Gentiles, which have not the law, do by nature the things contained in the law, these, having not the law, are a law unto themselves: Which shew the work of the law written in their hearts, their conscience also bearing witness, and their thoughts the mean while accusing or else excusing one another...

This passage has been seen principally as stating categorically that judgment for sin is not conditioned upon whether or not a person has heard the gospel or even known the law of God in the Bible, but rather upon doing what one knows, if only in his own conscience, to be wrong.

The startling truth of this verse when applied to our current subject of the spiritual condition of children is that until sin is consciously chosen, guilt for it is not held against children. Furthermore, Paul's denial of any difference between Jews and Gentiles with regard to guilt of sin means that the young children of complete pagans are no more subject to judgment than the children of two devout Christian parents, until the children themselves are old enough to sin consciously, and do so. If the grace of God covers children raised in a Christian home, it must also cover children raised in ignorance of Christian teaching.

Show me a verse

Some readers may want a more definitive verse. Why didn't Jesus or Paul just say, right up front, that very young children would go to heaven no matter what? Some may suggest that if there is no verse that actually says it, it can't be true. We must be careful not to subject all spiritual truths to such rigorous standards. Some religious groups deny the Trinity because there is no one verse that either uses the word "trinity" or says, 'God is one God in three persons.' Other groups declare that using pianos and organs in church is wrong because the Bible doesn't mention these instruments. Some theological certainties rely not on single verses but on a construction of several passages of scripture that beyond reasonable doubt lead to further conclusions.

Perhaps one reason the Holy Spirit didn't inspire a verse that explicitly taught the eternal security of very young children, or indeed a verse that might have explained an "age of accountability," was to keep us from laxness in child evangelism. A child innocent today may be responsible twenty-four hours from now. God secures children against condemnation until they can make moral choices, but Christians must remain vigilant in teaching the Bible and presenting Christ, ready to recognize the hour when our children cross over from innocence into accountability.

Looking at the scriptural indications of who lives in heaven raises the question of what happens there. More fundamentally, however, it suggests our inquiry into the very reason for heaven's existence.

Some people who question humanity's ubiquitous belief in a heavenly afterlife argue that there is no proof that heaven exists. They may deny the authenticity of the Bible as well as the rare experiences of people who claim to have glimpsed heaven. In these people's minds there is no reason to believe there is anything after this life. They may believe that human beings simply cease to exist.

Is there an answer to this sort of argument? We believe there is. Consider now the question of why there is a heaven.

4
WHY IS THERE A HEAVEN?

While the teachings of scripture are sufficient as a basis of our faith, we need not think that if scripture did not speak of a heaven, it would not therefore be reasonable to believe in it. In fact, we may *supplement* the revelation of God in the Bible with very simple, but quite powerful, inductive reasoning. Some universal experiences of human life fairly demand that we conclude that heaven exists.

Object of Instinctive Longing

Human beings are inclined to believe firmly in the existence of anything for which they perceive themselves to have an instinctive longing. Except for a few people (and they are, indeed, relatively few) who have convinced themselves that human life has no spiritual component and that there is no god whatsoever, otherwise humanity is distinctively marked by the universal longing for life beyond this life.

People want there to be a heavenly life after death. This longing is so strong, so prevalent and so pervasive that it may be regarded as instinctive to the human race. We are therefore powerfully drawn to induce that heaven does exist. We believe our longing for it is an internal indication that on a deep spiritual level we know already that heaven is a reality.

Examples from Nature

Human observation of animals leads to some fascinating

conclusions and even more fascinating mysteries. Why do salmon swim upstream to the place where they hatched, in order to spawn? Something is pre-programmed into their fishy brains to accomplish this feat, and despite the arduous nature of their journey they press on to accomplish it, knowing there is a place they must go and something they must do when they get there. They are not disappointed, because of course, there is such a place.

Even more puzzling, how do Monarch butterflies know where to migrate? The author lived in Fort Worth, Texas, for a few years and filmed untold thousands of Monarchs that used trees there as a way station on their southward journey.

Monarchs go through four generations in a year, three of them in northern climes in the U.S. The fourth generation, emerging from their pupas in September and October each year, migrates from all over America to either Southern California or Mexico, hibernating there until February or March. Then they return north. Three generations are born and die during the year before the next migration. How do the Monarchs that are metamorphosed from chrysalises and pupas in Missouri know to go to Mexico, and to feed on the same trees and hibernate in the same place their great-great-grandparents did? We have no explanation but instinct. They are pre-programmed to go, and the destination is as certain as their little longings to get there.

In some sense, human longings are more exalted than the instinctive urges of animals, but in another sense they seem just as primal, just as automatic, just as inescapable.

French philosopher Voltaire (François-Marie Arouet) is often quoted, even if the speaker or writer does not know or recall the source. Voltaire is famous for saying, "I disapprove of what you say, but I will defend to the death your right to say it." It was also he who said, "Common sense is not so common." On our topic, it was notably Voltaire who said, "If there were no God, it would have been necessary to invent him."

Voltaire's core reasoning was that something deep within the mind and soul of man demands that God exist. Man instinctively rests the reason of his existence on a purpose derived from a supreme being.

Similarly, since man knows there must be a God, other related concepts follow suit: there must be a realm where God exists and where human beings, in some form, can be united with him and know him more intimately. We sense that this world is a place of preparation or trial, marred by what we term human evil or sin, and that our sense or ability to perceive God while here is diminished and limited. Thus we conclude that heaven must exist because we long for it instinctively, *as a whole human race.*

This kind of inductive reasoning is not absent from the Bible. It is implied in a very important and striking verse from Hebrews. "Without faith it is impossible to please him: for he that cometh to God must believe that he is, and that he is a rewarder of them that diligently seek him" (Heb 11:6).

The Bible thus validates the instinctive belief people have that God exists. It goes further in revealing vital information we need to know in order to be certain that it is heaven we will experience instead of its dark and terrible alternative. The scripture promises further revelation of God and great blessing to us if we follow through with our natural hungering for him by seeking him with our whole hearts.

Answer to Mysteries of Life

Just as human beings inductively reason that heaven must exist because we persist as a race in longing for it, we also believe as a species that heaven exists because the mysteries of this life demand eventual answers.

Human beings overwhelmingly regard themselves as differing from the animals in the possession of a spiritual nature. This nature is an ability not only to be conscious of ourselves, which is the function of the human soul, but also to be conscious of God and to conceive of life beyond and apart from our immediate, physical surroundings. This is the function of the human spirit. This spiritual nature blesses us with an appreciation of our world and a sense of the divine, but it also plagues us with questions that seem to find no final and satisfactory answers.

We wonder about the overall purposes of God and our being on the earth. We wonder about the beginnings of everything that is. We wonder about the presence of evil in the human race. We ask ourselves why natural evils such as disasters take place in the world. We wonder why some innocent children die young and why some perversely evil people live to ripe old ages. We wonder why our wholesome purposes are so often thwarted. We ask ourselves often, whether we admit it or not, why God—if he can do anything—didn't prevent a terrible accident or a malicious deed. We wonder what really took place at seminal points in history, convinced that powerful people covered up terrible things, hoping they would never be revealed.

These and myriad other questions spin in our minds and hearts and generations of us have had them, asked them, pondered over them, and died with them unanswered. Can it really be that no answer to these questions of ours exists? Can it really be that our deepest and most intense wondering is not answered eventually?

Again, human beings inductively reason that their ability to ponder these deep questions and issues means that we have a spiritual nature that really belongs to another realm, another world, where the answers and explanations lie and will ultimately be given to us. This reasoning is what causes us to say casually, 'When I get to heaven, the first thing I'm going to ask God is..."

Justice for All

Americans are not alone in their quest to provide an atmosphere of governance where every citizen can expect justice. We have memorialized that goal in our Pledge of Allegiance. However, it is the intense desire of the peoples of the world to see justice done. Of all the questions the human race carries unanswered from generation to generation, those that deal with unpunished evil are the most pressing.

The Jews of Germany and surrounding countries during World War II certainly longed to see justice done, to each of them among the six million or so who were slaughtered by Hitler's Third Reich, and to all of them as a race, pestered and persecuted for thousands of years.

Christians for the past two millennia certainly have longed for justice. Burned, crucified and eaten by wild animals for sport, persecuted for believing in Jesus and in love, killed in droves by Muslims, murdered for doing missionary work and shot down by communist armies simply for being there, Christian martyrs probably outnumber those killed for any other social reason throughout history. Will anyone answer for this?

Nor is the issue of justice limited to redressing the persecution or killing of people of biblical faith. Vile injustice has taken place all over the world in pogroms directed at other people. Islam spread across the Middle East and Asia from the seventh to the thirteenth centuries largely by military conquest that included the slaughter of people who would not submit to the teachings of Muhammad. Communists in China imposed their will on other Asians, killing those who resisted.

African tribes throughout early history sought dominance over one another by unprovoked attack and mass slaughter. Slavery, not just in early America but in cultures around the world, has marred the histories of many nations. Genocide has been part of the conquest strategy of countless cultures throughout human history even before histories were ever written. Shall any of these terrible and unjust events ever be answered?

The human heart is urgent to conclude that eventually, somehow, all injustice will be answered, that evil will be repaid, and that righteousness will be rewarded after so long being delayed. This urgency forms itself into a spiritual certainty that justice will be done, in time, because God himself is just and will not allow injustice to prevail. For this reason we know instinctively there is a heaven.

The author is a magistrate and summary court judge handling matters of both civil and criminal nature. Among the most common criminal matters to come before his court are charges of fraudulent checks. State law prescribes what constitutes a *prima facie* case, and by the time a warrant is issued, the suspect is arrested, bond is set, and a trial date arrives, most defendants plead guilty. In bad check convictions, the court always issues two things: first, an order to make restitution to the victim; and second, a sentence consisting either of paying a fine or spending some days in jail. People almost always choose to pay the fine (imagine that!).

The sequence in which they comply with these orders is first that they must make restitution and show the court proof that they did; then, they must pay the fine, perhaps being allowed to do so over a period of weeks or months. A surprising number of people, however, seem to believe that once they have made restitution, they are free and clear. The court may have ordered them to repay their bad check for $750.00 and then pay a fine of $500.00. There always seem to be a few people who will show their receipt for $750.00 to the court and then argue with the court clerks that they shouldn't have to pay anything more.

In a completely reversed situation, some people convicted of bad checks may not make restitution at all, and the judge issues a bench warrant for their arrest. Once in jail, they may serve their thirty days or pay the fine originally imposed, and get out. Once out, a startling number of people believe that now that they have served their sentence, they have no obligation to the victim. Told by the court that they will be arrested again if they do not make restitution, they argue that they have already paid their debt, when they paid the fine. How can they not realize that they are still on the hook for stealing $750.00 from the person to whom they wrote a bad check?

The problem is that these people are thinking of justice only in one dimension, when there are, in fact, two. Justice is both a matter of those harmed being made whole, and also those who harmed them being punished. Both victim and victimizer must be repaid, each in kind.

This is the justice we human beings sense instinctively must be done, somehow, somewhere, sometime. Realizing that governments will never be able to provide complete justice for everyone living in their lands, and that untold injustices have gone by in the past without answer, we know, we just know, deep within us, that God will do justice to all. Heaven is our expectation of repayment for evil done to those doing good. Hell is our expectation of punishment to the evildoers themselves.

In addition to the great, natural yearning that convinces us of the reason there must be a heaven (and a corresponding hell), there are Bible revelations as to the purpose of heaven.

The Present Purpose

As our study has already revealed by answering the question of who will be in heaven, one of the most obvious purposes of heaven at the present time is as an abode for saints (all Christians) who die in this age. As opposed to any other waiting area, alternate destination, or state of sleep or suspended animation, heaven appears in scripture as the immediate destination of believers in Jesus Christ who die in this present, church age.

Abode for Saints who Die in this Age

As we have contended here, the overwhelming majority of human beings now and throughout history have longed for heaven and that longing serves as one source of evidence for heaven's existence. However, the longing of the entire race does not mean that everyone will go to the heaven we commonly conceive of. Heaven's purpose is as a destination for those who have a place reserved. There are qualifications for going to heaven.

The Bible is quite specific in explaining how people may be assured they will go to heaven.

> • Joh 3:16 - "For God so loved the world that he gave his only begotten Son, that whosoever believeth in him should not perish, but have everlasting life." This simplest of explanations of the Bible doctrine of salvation says that

a person must express and truly have faith and trust in Jesus Christ, the Son of God to have eternal life in heaven. This belief or trust is both in who Jesus is, the incarnate God the Son, and what Jesus did, having died for human sin and having been raised from the grave to never-ending life.

When Christians—whether preachers, evangelists, teachers or anyone communicating the gospel—ask others to accept or to receive Christ or to believe on Jesus Christ, they are inviting people to come to a decision. They are asking them to leave all other hopes of heaven behind, to turn from their former life and from disobedience to God, and to place their faith in Jesus Christ to be their Savior from sin and to give them a new birth of spiritual life that will result in their knowing Christ personally and being assured of a place in his heaven.

When the New Testament refers to "the saints," it means Christians—not just a few, notable Christians, but all Christians. The Greek word *hagios*, translated "saints," means "holy ones," and refers to all those made holy, or set apart, by the Lord Jesus as his people. It is these saints, all true Christians, *the saved,* who have reservations in heaven when they die in this age.

• Act 16:31 - "Believe on the Lord Jesus Christ, and thou shalt be saved." This terse summation of the apostolic invitation communicates the same information as Jesus' own formulation in Joh 3:16. The focus of salvation is Jesus Christ himself. Salvation is both an event changing life in the here and now, and an event securing our "reservations" in heaven.

• Joh 14:1-3 - "Let not your heart be troubled: ye believe in God, believe also in me. In my Father's house are many mansions: if it were not so, I would have told you. I go to prepare a place for you. And if I go and prepare a place for you, I will come again, and receive you unto myself; that where I am, there ye may be also." Jesus plainly taught his disciples that he would prepare a place for them all. Heaven exists as a place for those who follow Christ during this present age.

That Jesus said he would come again and receive his disciples unto himself has led some interpreters to suggest that followers of Christ who die in the present time will not immediately go to heaven. In the face of so much other evidence to the contrary, which we have seen in previous chapters, clearly Jesus did not mean there was any delay in a Christian's going to heaven upon death.

There seems rather to be a connection of Jesus' statement to his second coming and the general resurrection of the dead to take place at that juncture in history. While Christians will go to heaven upon their deaths, their form there probably will be a temporary embodiment, fully capable of experiencing everything in the heavenly realm, but not altogether or exactly what their bodies will be at the end of human history when Christ returns and the resurrection of the saints takes place.

This scriptural idea is further detailed by the Apostle Paul:

• 1Th 4:15-18 - "For this we say unto you by the word of the Lord, that we which are alive and remain unto the coming of the Lord shall not prevent [precede] them which are asleep. For the Lord himself shall descend from heaven with a shout, with the voice of the archangel, and with the trump of God: and the dead in Christ shall rise first: Then we which are alive and remain shall be caught up together with them in the clouds, to meet the Lord in the air: and so shall we ever be with the Lord. Wherefore comfort one another with these words."

Paul claimed to have this teaching directly from the Lord. Those he termed "asleep" are Christians who have died. He was not making a case for "soul sleep" or any such thing. His reference was to the bodies of the saints who have died. The Christian teaching of the resurrection of the dead is that when Christ returns, believers of all ages will be given or fitted with new resurrection bodies that are like Christ's body following his resurrection. Whatever temporary form we have following death in the present age, we will receive an "upgrade" at that time!

Paul didn't go into any detail as to what this enhanced, permanent, eternal form will be like, but certainly it has relevance to our subject of heavenly life, since we will experience eternity in these resurrection bodies. We will look at this subject further in the chapter on Life in Heaven.

Entrance is by physical death. The happy and welcome part of God's purpose for heaven is that Christians have a guarantee to be included in heaven's citizenry. Paul wrote in 2Co 5:4-5: "For we that are in this tabernacle do groan, being burdened: not for that we would be unclothed, but clothed upon, that mortality might be swallowed up of life. Now he that hath wrought us for the selfsame thing is God, who also hath given unto us the **earnest** of the Spirit" (emphasis ours). The word "earnest" in this verse means guarantee. The guarantee of reservations in heaven is the presence of the Holy Spirit in the Christian's life. Obviously this connection of the Spirit with assurance of heaven makes sensing the Holy Spirit's presence a very important part of Christian growth and living.

Unfortunately, the only way we have of entering heaven is

by the portal of physical death. This was not God's design in the beginning, but sin interrupted and altered that plan. The scriptures teach that "by one man sin entered into the world, and death by sin" (Rom 5:12). Great mystery surrounds the fact of death in the world, but we can be sure that sin is its ultimate cause.

While Christians anticipate the good things that will happen after death, dying itself is still not an event we commonly look forward to. For the most part, we do not know how we will die, whether in our sleep, which most people would desire, or by violence in excruciating pain, or something in between. It is the event we worry about, not its aftermath.

In part, what the assurance of our going to heaven is meant to do is alleviate excessive anxiety about dying itself. Jesus told Martha of Bethany, "I am the resurrection, and the life: he that believeth in me, though he were dead, yet shall he live: And whosoever liveth and believeth in me shall never die" (Joh 11:25-26). Jesus was challenging Martha to look *through* the moment and experience of death to what lay just beyond, and indeed, to look at life here and now as merely *continuing* through death and then going on forever. Knowing what comes after death changes the way we look at death itself.

Source of Visions and Aspirations

Heaven's purpose in this present age is not only as a destination and abode for Christians who die. It also serves as a source of visions and as an object of human aspirations.

Visions inspire us. When we read in the Bible about visions of heaven, they pique our interest in this ultimate destination. The information we garner from the typically scant details of ancient visions allows us tentatively to fill in some gaps in our knowledge of what heaven will be like.

Take for example the Transfiguration of Christ (Luk 9:28-36). This experience the disciples had, watching Jesus transformed before them into a heavenly form, fits into the general category of a vision, but we must be careful to note that it was not a dream or any other sort of representative experience. They actually did see their Master and two other persons in a heavenly setting, somehow coincident with that particular location on the mountain where they were. There was an intersection of the heavenly and earthly realms for a few moments and they were privy to what few people on earth ever have been. The source for this vision was heaven itself, rather than some dramatic construction more like a divinely produced movie shown to a sleeping mind.

The salient facts we can draw from this amazing and memorable event for the disciples have to do with the interaction of people and God in heaven. Luke's account said that once he was transfigured, Jesus began conversing with Moses and Elijah. In itself, this very likely tells us that saints of all the ages will be able to (and now presently do) know and converse with each other. The obvious further implication is that people in heaven have no difficulty recognizing one another. A second observation we may make easily is that conversation with Jesus himself will be possible. That Moses and Elijah were major figures in the national history of Israel should not be taken to indicate that there was or is any fraternity of the elite in heaven. Remember that Jesus himself said of John the Baptist, "Among them that are born of women there hath not risen a greater than John the Baptist: notwithstanding he that is least in the kingdom of heaven is greater than he" (Mat 11:11).

It is probably reasonable to conclude as well from the Transfiguration that heaven's citizens now have a fundamental awareness of what is going on at a general level on the earth. Moses and Elijah were aware of the plan of redemption being worked out in the life of the incarnate Son. Perhaps this was an exceptional event of which all heaven was informed, but probably it is not a stretch to guess that people in heaven are aware of the general progress of the gospel, periods of intense persecution, and so on.

Parenthetically, we should note that neither from this verse nor any similar reference are we justified in concluding that people in heaven may casually observe life on earth. The notion that our loved ones watch over us, as if they were angels, or view us in our tragedies or triumphs, is not biblical. Some who hold this view may call on Heb 12:1 with its reference to "so great a cloud of witnesses" as a biblical basis for such a belief. However, the author of Hebrews was not arguing that the historical figures whose exploits of faith he recounted in Heb 11 now sit in heaven watching life on earth. Either he meant they were witnesses of the Christian church in a historical and metaphorical sense, or he meant they were witnesses in their own times to the validity of faith in God as the divinely approved way to live. As for the sensibleness of people in heaven being able to watch us as we live on earth, one has only to press the notion to its logical extreme to realize how tedious or even voyeuristic such watching could be, to conclude that the idea is ludicrous.

As another example of inspiration consider the vision given to Stephen just before he was stoned (Act 7:54-56). From the description, it appears that the vision was to Stephen alone, but he described what he was seeing, which enabled the Christian community to preserve the event and ultimately to commit it to writing. Stephen saw heaven, the Glory of God, and Jesus standing on the right hand of God. Other than the confirmation of the visible glory of God in heaven we are also treated to an image of Jesus Christ, not seated, but *standing* at the right hand of God the Father.

This unique event in scripture has inspired Christians to an awareness that Christ himself honors the courage and sacrifice of his witnesses on earth. Jesus is not a passive observer of what his followers are doing in this physical realm, but rather an active Lord engaging with them by his Spirit and upholding them and honoring them as they serve him. This fact is an inspiration to Christians everywhere to follow faithfully and pay whatever price they must to be Christ's ambassadors, and if necessary, his martyrs. The source of this inspiration was a vision from heaven.

Visions teach us. Occasionally, visions teach us directly. Particularly speaking of biblical visions, sometimes God used brief windows on heaven to give specific information that became a constructive part of our theological knowledge.

At Jesus' baptism, a vision took place that Jesus witnessed. The record we have of the event says that when Jesus came up out of the water, "lo, the heavens were opened unto him, and he saw the Spirit of God descending like a dove, and lighting upon him: and lo a voice from heaven, saying, This is my beloved Son, in whom I am well pleased" (Mat 3:16-17). Luke's version says "Thou art my beloved Son," as if Jesus alone heard the voice. Matthew and Mark both record a remembrance that the voice said, "This"—the third person pronoun— suggesting that others heard the voice. The details of how the fact of, or the content of, the vision was transmitted to the disciples are not given.

What is significant about the vision, however, is that God the Father used this brief intersection of heaven with earth to identify Jesus as the incarnate Son. Jesus would make this claim himself later, and he would demonstrate this fact in numerous ways, but here at the outset of his ministry a vision was the means of teaching both the disciples and every person who would ever read the gospel accounts, that Jesus of Nazareth was the Son of God.

In another extended example, almost all of the Revelation to John is an account of a vision or a series of visions consisting of scenes set in heaven. Much of what the Christian church knows to expect about the second coming of Christ was depicted in the visions of Revelation. Here again, visions of heaven have the purpose of teaching. We will look at a portion of John's vision of heaven in greater detail in an upcoming chapter.

A third example of significant teaching material contained in a vision of heaven is found in an experience of the Apostle Peter in Acts. Peter was on a housetop in Joppa praying before lunch and Luke recorded that "he fell into a trance, and saw heaven opened." What followed was the vision of a sheet knit at the four corners let down to earth, containing miscellaneous animals. Peter heard a voice tell him to kill some of the animals and eat them, and he declined, saying he had never eaten unclean foods—clearly he recognized the assortment as forbidden game. The voice replied that Peter was not to call anything unclean that God has cleansed (Act 10:11-15).

The entire scene repeated itself three times and then the sheet went back into heaven and Peter was jerked back into the everyday world. He instantly realized what the import of the vision was. God was teaching him that no more should he reserve his fellowship and his message for his Jewish brethren only. From then on he was to include Gentiles in the gospel and in the church.

We should consider the question of whether Peter's vision was a projection of God's message into his mind, or an actual view of something being played out in heaven itself. If the latter, obviously a drama was being presented for Peter's consideration. More likely we should regard the vision as a set of scenes delivered to the mind and heart of Peter from the Holy Spirit. The "heaven" opened in v.11, however, appears in context to have been not just the sky, but the heaven of God.

Therefore, the question of whether the vision was a direct view of heaven or a representation of heaven becomes virtually irrelevant. Either way, God was using heavenly scenes to transmit vital teaching to his church. The message was the universality of the gospel. For some two millennia God's revelation had come to the Israelites, who were to keep themselves separate from other peoples in many ways. Now God used a vision to make crystal clear that his arms were open wide to everyone on earth who would hear and believe the gospel.

As an illustration of the virtual absence of difference between seeing heaven for real or seeing a series of divinely projected images in the mind and heart, consider another illustration from court. In some murder cases, some evidence may be too gory for many jurors to view without being unnecessarily distracted or even prejudiced by it. Sometimes an artist's rendering is substituted for photographs, with the approval of the judge. In fact, drawings are occasionally clearer to interpret than photographs for a variety of reasons. While the photos were captures of the actual scene, the drawings are a step removed. Even the photos, however, were not direct, live views of the murder. The point is that the original event is what is communicated, even if by derivative, representational means.

A vision of heaven, then, need not be an actual, real-time view of what's going on in heaven. The fact that the vision emanates from heaven—from the mind of God—defines it as heavenly in source. The Lord has used such heavenly visions to teach his saints vital truths.

Since the writing of the New Testament documents and the acceptance of the canon of the New Testament in A.D. 325, numerous Christians have reported having visions, some of them specifically of heavenly sights. If we include the category of NDEs, we would have a sizeable body of reports of heavenly visions. It is possible that some of these visions were useful to the wider Christian community in the way of inspiration or teaching, though it is more likely that their value was in the effects they had on the persons experiencing them.

However, Christians must be careful about casually accepting claims of visions, especially where the reports or the implications of what people say they saw tend to conflict with New Testament teaching or add new information or instruction that goes beyond the fixed body of New Testament writings. Remember that cults and essentially non-Christian offshoots have arisen based on radical "visions." The Mormon Church and Seventh Day Adventists can be traced to seminal visions by their founders, as can cults such as that of David Koresh. There is good reason for being satisfied with the visions of heaven reported in the pages of scripture. We can be certain those accounts will not mislead us.

Two millennia have gone by since the life, death and resurrection of Jesus. Untold millions of people have heard the gospel, become Christians, lived their lives following Christ, and died in the Lord. They have gone to heaven, one by one, during generation after generation, through century after century, fulfilling the purpose of heaven for this present age.

For many people, there seems no end in sight to the march

of time. Things get better or worse, wars are fought and ended, nations rise and fall, technology apparently advances without retreat, and while every now and then there is a resurgence of predictions of imminent doom of some kind, life continues as the doomsayers are discredited. On the basis of this pattern, some people assume that there will be no interruption, no dramatic shift, no end, no new beginning.

The Apostle Peter noted that people in his day made this assumption, and he said it was a grave mistake:

> Knowing this first, that there shall come in the last days scoffers, walking after their own lusts, And saying, Where is the promise of his coming? for since the fathers fell asleep, all things continue as they were from the beginning of the creation. (2Pe 3:3-4)

Peter went on to comment further on the folly of the belief that there would be no end of the world simply because things looked like they would go on and on without interruption. We note first, however, that he called this assumption the conclusion of scoffers who were busy filling their lives with worldly cravings. In other words, it suited people of degenerate living to believe that they would never answer for their wrongs.

Christians, however, as we have seen, have a longing for heaven as the justice of God, for rewarding those who follow Christ. Heaven's converse is hell, designed for delivering God's justice with regard to those who have persecuted the godly and perpetuated evil of all kinds in this life. The scriptures go further, however. Not only are Christians able with confidence to expect a heavenly destination in this present age for each individual follower of Christ who dies, but at some point in human history, as a shock to those who have dismissed the possibility and a welcome surprise to those who have anticipated it, Jesus Christ is going to come back to earth.

The second coming of Christ is the biblically prophesied time that generally refers to a cluster of events bringing the present age to a close, establishing the unexceptional reign of Christ over the world, and changing the configuration of life for eternity. We turn now in our study to these end-time events. They will result in a dramatic change in the relationship and juxtaposition of heaven to earth.

5
Heaven on Earth

In the Scottish play—what superstitious thespians prefer to call Shakespeare's *Macbeth*—three witches tell Macbeth that he need not worry about being discovered in his murder of King Duncan in order to succeed him. One of the apparitions tells him, "Macbeth shall never vanquish'd be until Great Birnam wood to high Dunsinane hill Shall come against him." Well, Birnam wood was several miles from Dunsinane, and Macbeth figured that forests did not move. He felt reassured that he had gotten away with his crime.

Unfortunately for Macbeth, armies moving against him came through Birnam wood and cut large branches to camouflage themselves, moving slowly across the land, a forest creeping toward Dunsinane. When Macbeth's soldiers realized what was happening, it was too late to prevent their defeat.

As surprising as it might seem to the average person learning of Bible prophesies, while heaven and earth seem removed from each other by a fixed distance or dimension, the time will come when heaven will come to earth, and the two will meet.

The phrase, "heaven on earth," has been used to describe countries, states, restaurants, day spas, furniture and clothing, to name just a few things. The Church of Jesus Christ of Latter Day Saints describes the ideal home as heaven on earth. The concept is cheapened by some of its applications, but there really will be a heaven on earth someday, and it could be very soon.

Various Bible prophecies describe events that have come to be known generally as the end times, what theologians call the *eschaton,* the Greek word for "last things." Students of the Bible know that the end times include some or all of the following, not necessarily in this exact order: the tribulation sometimes divided into two parts; the rapture of the church; the second coming of Christ, sometimes seen in two stages; a millennial reign of Christ, variously positioned with respect to these other items; the resurrection of the dead in Christ; the resurrection of the unsaved dead; the judgment of the unsaved; the re-creation of earth and heaven; and the appearance of the New Jerusalem in heaven. The image that arises out of the many Bible prophecies touching on the end times is of a rapid series of events, at least compared to the length of human history, resulting in an altered plane of existence for everyone.

The scope of our study cannot include a comprehensive investigation of all these prophecies. We are specifically interested in discovering what the Bible teaches about what happens in heaven, or to heaven, when the end times come.

Earth and Heaven Re-created

When Peter wrote what he did in 2Pe 3:13 by inspiration from the Holy Spirit, he gave us an important, fascinating, exciting new piece of information not just about life beyond the grave, but also about life beyond this present age.

> ...Looking for and hasting unto the coming of the day of God, wherein the heavens being on fire shall be dissolved, and the elements shall melt with fervent heat... Nevertheless we, according to his promise, look

for new heavens and a new earth, wherein dwelleth righteousness (2Pe 3:12-13).

This prophecy fits nicely with the implications of Paul's statement in Romans that both we and the world we live in will be redeemed somehow from the corruption that prevails in so many ways in creation at this moment:

> For I reckon that the sufferings of this present time are not worthy to be compared with the glory which shall be revealed in us. For the earnest expectation of the creature waiteth for the manifestation of the sons of God. For the creature was made subject to vanity, not willingly, but by reason of him who hath subjected the same in hope, Because the creature itself also shall be delivered from the bondage of corruption into the glorious liberty of the children of God. For we know that the whole creation groaneth and travaileth in pain together until now. And not only they, but ourselves also, which have the firstfruits of the Spirit, even we ourselves groan within ourselves, waiting for the adoption, to wit, the redemption of our body (Rom 8:18-23).

Paul's position on the cause and effect of sin on God's creation included not only death as a primary byproduct, but miscellaneous other results comprehended in his phrase, "the bondage of corruption." This bondage resulted in the entire creation's groaning and travailing in pain, and consequently waiting for redemption.

Earth without Violence

The effects of sin on the creation may be logically inferred to include violence in the natural order, predation and suffering, as well as death. This conclusion is supported by a much older prophecy, that of Isaiah:

> The wolf also shall dwell with the lamb, and the leopard shall lie down with the kid; and the calf and the young lion and the fatling together; and a little child shall lead them (Isa 11:6).

Isaiah was looking forward in time to the end of the age of sin's reign. He fully anticipated that when God set things right in the world and brought his sovereign and beneficent rule to bear in creation, all violence would cease. He specifically illustrated his point with the classic violence of wolves, leopards and lions against lambs, kid goats and calves.

It is reasonable for us to ask ourselves whether or not Isaiah meant his readers to understand his words literally. Was he saying that after God brought judgment and justice to his creation, there would continue to be animals of all kinds just as now, and yet no predation, no carnivores, no hunters or killers in the entire animal kingdom? The larger point of Isaiah's prophecy is certainly that while war, strife, animosity, threats, danger and fear are everyday realities in this age, peace will reign supreme in the age to come. Lions and lambs, etc., are symbols of that peace, pictured as they are by Isaiah as curled up with each other like friendly pets on a fireside rug.

Does the use of the symbol, however, eliminate any other meaning? One reason to believe that Isaiah was giving us illustrations from his envisionment of the actual circumstances of the future earth is his inclusion of the idea that little children will lead around what are now vicious animals. There would seem to be no great symbolism in the statement that "a little child shall lead them." A literal interpretation is therefore favored.

Isaiah gave two other striking illustrations of how harmless everything will be:

> And the sucking child shall play on the hole of the asp, and the weaned child shall put his hand on the cockatrice' den. (Isa 11:8).

These images intensify the concept of there being no violence by animals to man, an idea that has little to no symbolic significance but rather appears to be an expectation of the actual shape of nature.

Isaiah further emphasized the actuality of his predictions by the repetition of such images later in his works:

> The wolf and the lamb shall feed together, and the lion shall eat straw like the bullock: and dust shall be the serpent's meat. They shall not hurt nor destroy in all my holy mountain, saith the Lord (Isa 65:25).

Not only did Isaiah repeat his imagery of the wolf and lamb being "friends," he gave his readers the other side of the equation, so to speak, in telling them what predators would do instead of eating other animals. Lions would eat hay and snakes would "eat dirt." Many of us would agree this seems appropriate for snakes!

There is no symbolism in stating that animals that are carnivorous now will be herbivorous in the future. We can reasonably conclude, then, that Isaiah meant to say that the animal kingdom will actually be revolutionized after that point in history we have come to know as the end times.

Such a scenario seems unlikely or incredible to most of us.

We have never known a world in which anything but a food chain of animals is the rule. The evolutionary model for life on earth, which dominates public school teaching in our times, says that from the time of anything more complex than single-celled creatures, predation has been the pattern of the animal kingdom. In other words, what almost everyone is taught in school reinforces the belief that nature without violence is impossible.

We should take careful note, however, of the larger belief system of the typical evolutionist position. Most scientists who rigorously hold to the evolution of life on earth also: deny the existence of God or his involvement in the world; reject the virgin birth; do not believe in an incarnate God; do not believe in resurrection from the dead; reject divine healing; and dismiss other things that are *intimately and necessarily* part of the Bible record. If we doubt the eventuality of a natural order in which there is no food chain of animals, we are probably buying into the world's denial of the reality of supernatural beings and events altogether.

In recent times a number of stories about unlikely friendships between people and normally vicious animals have made news. Some years ago Anthony "Ace" Bourke and John Rendall, two Australians, reared a lion as a pet and more recently had a reunion with him, which they filmed. The lion acted like a pussycat as he recognized them and "hugged" them. George Adamson of "Born Free" fame is another person who had peaceful and affectionate friendships with several lions. A South African, Kevin Richardson, kept a preserve with as many as thirty-eight lions with whom he lolled and played. We marvel at videos of such sights, but they serve to prove that what we rationally fear as enemies could be welcomed as friends under different circumstances.

Even evolutionists concede that carnivores can become

herbivores over time, and the animal kingdom at the present time includes some species that eat vegetation or other animals, depending on the availability of the food source. Why should we think it incredible that the shape of the future is a world without violence between species?

The Bible's teaching that Christians can expect new heavens and a new earth is a major part of the coming dynamic change in the relationship of earth to heaven. For not only do the scriptures foretell a radical change in the interaction of biological life, they also give us a peek at the new accessibility of the heavenly realm to everything in the physical universe we know.

Heaven No Longer Beyond Us

A clear concept of how the earth we know will be renovated with some striking differences is an important realization. For the world will be fitted or readied for the changes that will take place with regard to heaven.

In the present age, heaven is beyond us. It is a dimension that we cannot access by any means known to us while our bodies are living. At his own initiative, God has opened doors upon heaven on rare occasions, but otherwise we cannot experience it in any way until we die. The spiritual part of us, which has, so to speak, a foot in the heavenly realm, must separate from our bodies and enter the spiritual dimension. Heaven is remote, in that sense. This is the world we know and anything else is a matter of faith and anticipation.

All that is going to change. In a remarkable foretelling of the future, the book of Revelation informs us that God is going to turn the present order of things on its head.

The Apostle John recorded in Joh 14:1-4 that Jesus told us, by way of telling his disciples, that *he* takes *us* to be with him in this present age as we die. But in Rev 21:1-2, John said *God* is going to come to *us*. While now we anticipate going to heaven, eventually heaven is going to come to us.

> And I saw a new heaven and a new earth: for the first heaven and the first earth were passed away; and there was no more sea. And I John saw the holy city, new Jerusalem, coming down from God out of heaven, prepared as a bride adorned for her husband. And I heard a great voice out of heaven saying, Behold, the tabernacle of God is with men, and he will dwell with them, and they shall be his people, and God himself shall be with them, and be their God (Rev 21:1-3).

This passage of scripture gives us an exciting preview of a future event, the descent of a heavenly place into the visible realm of earth. The word "new" describing Jerusalem, heaven and earth, is *kainos* in the Greek, which means recently made or fresh, and of a new kind. It is a *different* Jerusalem being described, not the old Jerusalem now in the Holy Land. It is a different earth, as the previous predictions concerning the animal kingdom made clear. It is also a new heaven, for in some respects heaven will be fundamentally altered.

John noted in his vision in Rev 21 that he saw no sea. All the major scholarly commentators on this passage agree that the sea is a symbol of separation between God and man. This meaning is confirmed by v. 3, which explains that God intends in the future to establish a much more visible, evidential presence with his people than now exists, since now he is invisible to us in this world.

To be consistent with our previous method, however, we must ask whether or not the statement that "there was no sea" is meant entirely symbolically. Specifically, if we take the new heaven and the new earth to be actual, shouldn't we take "no sea" to be an actual prediction as well?

To begin with, it is vital that we note that John did not say, 'there were no more seas,' but "no more sea," in the singular. Some modern versions have "any sea," but this is a loose translation. The Greek has the little word *ouk,* which means simply "not." The word for sea in this passage, *thalassa,* means a particular sea, most often in the Bible the Red Sea or the Mediterranean Sea. It also means lake, as in the Sea of Galilee, which is also known as the Lake of Gennesaret or Lake Tiberias. John knew of what we call the Indian Ocean and of the sea that lay on the other side of Gibraltar. If he had meant to say that the vision he saw precluded the existence of any bodies of water anywhere, certainly he would have said 'seas' instead of using the singular.

Nevertheless, he did remark that he didn't see a sea in his vision. Since the vision was of the new earth and heaven, it would seem likely that he was comparing what he saw to his knowledge of the Mediterranean Sea as the western border of Israel. The new earth he saw lacked any such sea. Some large body of water that was associated particularly with the idea of separation or isolation was no longer there, in John's vision.

Nothing would prevent God's planning the re-creation of earth in such a way that no oceans remain, of course, but other than the symbolic significance of God's removing separation from us and him, there would seem to be no purpose in eliminating oceans from earth, whether from the existing earth if it is re-formed, or a new earth entirely if God replaces this one. Indeed, unless God were to change physics for the entire universe, which isn't anywhere implied in the scripture, eliminating oceans would probably make even the *new* earth uninhabitable.

What if John were trying to communicate the idea that God left something out of the new earth that was universally feared or disliked, as the viciousness of animals is feared by all of us? If the sea were feared by all, one could understand eliminating it. However, while some people now find the sea daunting and dangerous, others love it and are enchanted by it. Have you ever found yourself smiling at the image of a cruise ship with a backdrop of a golden sunset over a landless horizon? Have you ever spent a glorious day on a beach fishing, swimming, or just listening to the surf, content to be doing nothing else?

As we will comment on some other features of heaven to be described shortly in John's vision, some of the images he saw had a degree of literalness to them but an even greater degree of symbolism, not meant to be forced beyond the bounds of reason.

The greater point of this specific revelation to John was, of course, the new relationship of God to man. Heaven was coming to earth because God was coming to man in a historically unprecedented manner. "He will dwell with them, and they shall be his people, and God himself shall be with them, and be their God" (Rev 21:3).

Of the various longings of people who have come to faith in Jesus Christ and begun to learn who God is, probably none is more intense or increases more over the years than the desire to experience the presence of God and of Jesus Christ the Son with greater reality. Like Moses, we want to say to God, "Show me thy glory!" (Exo 33:18). Like the Greeks who approached Philip the disciple, "We would see Jesus." Like the disciple Thomas, we want to touch his hands, not to change doubt into belief, but to glory in his saving love.

These fond desires will be fulfilled when heaven comes to earth. In some way, while this age continues, they will be fulfilled when we breathe our last in this world and go to be with the Lord. In a greater way, once God breaks into history to change it altogether, our hope of seeing and knowing God the Father, Son and Spirit will be thoroughly fulfilled. This was the true import of John's vision of the new Jerusalem in Revelation 21.

Life without Sorrow or Death

Along with the Christian's great yearning to see and know God intimately, a nearly universal desire of humanity is to live in a place where there is perfect joy and peace, and where people never grow infirm or die. The Christian has, in the revelations given to "holy men of God" (2Pe 1:21), promises that when heaven comes to earth, such a perfect place will be the permanent home of the redeemed in Christ.

> He will wipe every tear from their eyes. There will be no more death or mourning or crying or pain, for the old order of things has passed away (Rev 21:4).

This verse, which is heard in probably 99% of all grave side messages delivered by evangelical pastors, is a summation of all the negative emotions and experiences of mankind. There was no need for John to extend his list to include every variation. We understand him to be saying that in the world that is coming, no sorrow, regret, guilt, self-recrimination, hurt, shame, depression, fear, or any other thing that diminishes peace, enjoyment, or love, will be experienced ever again.

Anticipating such a time and such a life is deeply exciting. When we think through the promise, however, we cannot avoid the question of how life in heaven, or heaven on earth, can be without certain negatives. What will change that no sorrow will interrupt life? What will be different so that no regret comes to mind?

Absence of Sin and Evil

First of all, in the age when heaven comes to earth, no sin will exist. Though all human beings now sin (Rom 3:23), none who enter into God's heaven will ever sin again. The sinful nature will be thoroughly removed and the spirit of every human being will be right with God. The tempter will not be allowed access to creation anymore, so there will be no temptation. With no sin, no one will hurt anyone in any way, either physically or emotionally. The reign of love will mean that human interactions will never give anyone reason to feel resentment, fear, anger, or any other negative thing. These conclusions are the direct and necessary result of there being "no more...crying or pain." Sinful acts by sinful beings cause others crying and pain. The absence of the effect demands the absence of the cause.

Further, no disease, infirmity, injury, degeneration or death will exist. Though all human beings now die (Heb 9:27), none who enter into God's heaven will ever die again. The very meaning of eternal or everlasting life is that it continues without end. The fundamental change that will take place as a result of the resurrection will alter the nature of our existence in the new heaven and new earth, because "the dead shall be raised incorruptible, and we shall be changed" (1Co 15:52). No cause of disease or death will exist; therefore, no effect will take place.

Isaiah's prophecy underscored this same expectation. He wrote, "They shall not hurt nor destroy in all my holy mountain: for the earth shall be full of the knowledge of the Lord, as the waters cover the sea." (Isa 11:6-9). Not only will the re-creation of the earth result in the pacification of the animal kingdom, it will also result in the removal of all anger and violence from human hearts. No one will hurt anyone else, ever.

Isaiah gave the reason for this universal benevolence as being that the earth would be full of the knowledge of the Lord. This knowledge will certainly be more than factual information. It is a knowledge that includes an understanding of the heart and mind of God to the limits of each creature's ability to possess it. Paul the Apostle had this kind of knowledge in mind when he wrote that his goal was "that I may know him, and the power of his resurrection, and the fellowship of his sufferings, being made conformable unto his death" (Phi 3:10). Paul wanted to know Christ in such a way that he would be like him in this world. In other words, he associated the knowledge of Christ with the imitation of Christ. The same will be true in the new heavens and earth as to the knowledge of God. Knowing him as fully as possible will result in our reflecting his goodness and justice without exception.

Human beings can never know God completely since he is infinitely beyond our ability to comprehend. However, in our present state we are possessed of a paltry ability to know him, due to the effects of sin on our minds and hearts. In the re-creation of the earth and through the transformation that will come in the resurrection of the saints, we will be rid of sin and its effects and will acquire the ability to know God as fully as possible for who and what we are.

The absence of sin and evil from the world to come is a fairly obvious conclusion drawn from both Old and New Testament prophecies. What isn't so obvious is why there will still be no sorrow in view of the many circumstances in this present world that might provoke it.

Perfect Rule of Peace

What will eliminate the occurrence of any sorrow, regret, depression, hopelessness or any other negative spirit in the new heaven and earth is the perfect rule of God's peace in every resurrected human being.

Christians often wonder whether, when they get to heaven, they will remember their lives on earth, either fully or in part. For some people, the assurance that there will be no "mourning or crying or pain" demands that they have either no memory, or only selective memory, of their earthly lives. They anticipate that they would feel regret for many things done or not done. Further, and perhaps most troubling to many Christians, they wonder how they will be able to avoid experiencing sorrow when they go to heaven but unsaved friends, parents, children, siblings or even spouses do not. How, they wonder, would they be able to enjoy heaven when someone they loved so much on this side of eternity would suddenly and forever be removed from them?

This is no light matter, and the troubling question people have about it cannot be dismissed. There is an answer to it, however. The answer lies first in settling the issue of whether or not we will recall our lives here, and to what extent.

Recalling life. There is no concrete evidence for holding that in heaven we will have no memory of earth. What scriptures there are that speak of forgetting the past refer to God, not man. Jer 31:34 says that God will "remember their sin no more," but clearly this is a position God takes toward our pasts rather than his loss of recollection. There is no implication in this verse about any corresponding inability of human beings to remember their own sins. Heb 8:12 and 10:17 make the same statement as Jeremiah and mean the same thing.

The statement in Rev 21:4 presents us with a reason for the absence of sorrow in heaven: "for the former things are passed away." Some take passing away to mean no longer in memory. However, this inference is not warranted by the language used. The Greek word translated "passed away" literally means "came from," and implies a complete change of scene or place as a result of travel or transposition. Going to heaven is a permanent relocation, from a place filled with *active* causes for sorrow to a place with no such active causes at all. Whether or not this passing away implies that memories of earth will be removed from us by God is a question that must be answered by other evidence.

The most powerful evidence that we will remember our earthly lives is the fact that in heaven we will be cognizant of the great cost of our salvation in Jesus Christ and the reason that he had to suffer and die if we were to be saved. If we had no memory of our lives we would have no memory of having sinned, and in that condition we would have no *informed appreciation* of what Christ did on our behalf.

John's vision in Rev 5 seems definitive concerning the memory of earth's life—certainly of the profound impact of sin and the priceless nature of Jesus' sacrifice:

> And they sung a new song, saying, Thou art worthy to take the book, and to open the seals thereof: for thou wast slain, and hast redeemed us to God by thy blood out of every kindred, and tongue, and people, and nation; And hast made us unto our God kings and priests: and we shall reign on the earth. And I beheld, and I heard the voice of many angels round about the throne and the beasts and the elders: and the number of them was ten thousand times ten thousand, and thousands of thousands; Saying with a loud voice, Worthy is the Lamb that was slain to receive power, and riches, and wisdom, and strength, and honour, and

glory, and blessing (Rev 5:9-12).

In heaven, our understanding of the saving work of Christ will continue to be, as it is now, predicated on our awareness of the sin that marked our lives here. Only in this awareness will we find the depth of God's mercy and grace in sending himself in the person of Jesus Christ to die for us. This awareness does not mean we will be obsessed with the memory, only that the memory will not be erased.

To be sure, in the presence of God there will be reason enough to exalt and praise him, simply for who he is, quite apart from any specific awareness of things we have done. The angels in heaven have no sin and yet they praise God. Worship of God and of Jesus Christ will be motivated by the sheer fact of his deity and glory. However, the specific mention in Rev 5 of our glorifying God for being redeemed means we will understand the reason for our having needed redemption.

There is further scriptural evidence, quite strong in itself, that we will recall our lives on earth. Consider the following scriptures:

- Luk 16:19-31 – Jesus' story about the rich man and Lazarus shows us two people who went in different directions upon death. The rich man looked up from hell and recognized Lazarus in heaven, as well as Abraham. A skeptical interpreter might suggest that it would be logical to assume that people in hell would remember their lives because it would be part of their punishment that they would exist with infinite regret. The same position would suggest that by contrast people in heaven would forget their lives so as to have no reason to regret at all.

  However, more scriptures add to the evidence for our

memory of earth.

- 1Th 2:19 – "For what is our hope, or joy, or crown of rejoicing? Are not even ye in the presence of our Lord Jesus Christ at his coming? For ye are our glory and joy." Paul fully expected to know his converts when they all got to heaven. How would he know they were converts of his, or know them at all, if upon going to heaven everyone forgets earth? Paul's unwritten assumption in this verse is that heaven's residents will recognize previous acquaintances.
- 1Th 4:17 – "Then we which are alive and remain shall be caught up together with them in the clouds, to meet the Lord in the air: and so shall we ever be with the Lord." This verse adds further weight to the argument that our consciousness of ourselves and others in heaven will be a continuation of our consciousness of life just before we die. Paul was dealing with the concern of the Thessalonian believers about whether or not they would see their loved ones who had preceded them in death. His assurance was that each in his order would rise and then that all of the saved would be together with the Lord. It is unthinkable to draw a conclusion that loved ones who will be with the Lord will not know one another. On the contrary, Paul's encouragement to his readers to "Comfort one another with these words" (1Th 4:18) is based on his assumption of our continued memory of one another's lives when we arrive in heaven.
- Mat 17:4 – "Lord, it is good for us to be here: if thou wilt, let us make here three tabernacles; one for thee, and one for Moses, and one for Elias." The disciples saw the transfiguration of Christ and recognized Moses and Elijah, though they had not been contemporaries. Doubtless there were no paintings of them, either! There may have

been visual clues of some other kind, but the point is that they knew who these two people were.

• Mat 8:11 – "And I say unto you, That many shall come from the east and west, and shall sit down with Abraham, and Isaac, and Jacob, in the kingdom of heaven." The unspoken premise of this prophecy is that redeemed human beings of all generations will have knowing fellowship with each other. Who they were on earth, and who we were, will matter.

Our recognition in heaven of each other and of the nature of our relationships and friendships is the corollary of our remembering our own earthly lives. Unless we suppose that God will selectively remove our memory of unsaved friends and family—for which there is no evidence—we must conclude that we will remember those we knew and perhaps loved, who did not accept the gift of eternal life in Christ.

Since we will remember ourselves and others from this life, it is an inescapable conclusion that we will recall our sins as well as our Christlike living.

Experiencing peace. If our memories of our lives and the lives of others will not be selectively purged, how then will we be able to avoid feeling grief, regret and pain? The answer lies in our premise statement at the beginning of this section. The perfect rule of God's peace will eliminate any negative response in us to our memories.

The power of the peace of God is vastly underestimated by many Christians. Many believers think they could not tolerate some circumstance, condition, difficulty, tragedy, injustice or even some terrible knowledge, and maintain their equilibrium or their hope. The key to the Christian's facing the troubles of this life is the peace of God.

Numerous scriptures speak of the gift of peace.

- Joh 16:33 – "These things I have spoken unto you, that in me ye might have peace." While Jesus said his disciples would have tribulation in the world, his answer and remedy was peace, his peace, the peace of God. In the world to come, this peace will be unimpeded, uninhibited, invincible.
- Gal 5:22 – "But the fruit of the Spirit is love, joy, peace…" Peace is the natural result of living in harmony with the plan of God by being led by the Holy Spirit. While we experience times of spiritual filling and great peace here, in the hereafter the Spirit of God will have perfect fruit in all heaven's residents and his peace will envelop every soul.
- Rom 5:1 – "Being justified by faith, we have peace with God through our Lord Jesus Christ." The fear people have of dying and of eternity's justice is completely allayed once Jesus Christ comes to be Lord. In heaven, after we have received the final aspect of our redemption, that peace we had on earth will be complete and will not be able to be disturbed.
- Isa 26:3 – "Thou wilt keep him in perfect peace, whose mind is stayed on thee: because he trusteth in thee." In this world, when the mind loses its focus on the One who alone fulfils the heart, doubt, fear, worry, regret and other debilitating attitudes creep in. Peace that controls perfectly also eliminates these negatives. Our peace in heaven will be flawless.
- Luk 24:36 – "Peace be unto you." To disciples plagued by fear and uncertainty Jesus bequeathed his own peace. Surely the peace of Jesus is perfect, and however consistently experienced here by us, it will be uninterrupted in its influence upon us when we go to heaven.

- Rom 8:6 – "To be spiritually minded is life and peace." While we are variously successful in being spiritually minded while on earth, in heaven we will never be anything else but spiritually minded, i.e., fully in tune with the Spirit of God, and therefore our peace will be imperturbable.
- Col 3:15 – "Let the peace of God rule in your hearts." God's peace is not merely an attribute; it is a ruling attitude, a perspective on people and events, and a state of mind and heart determining our responses. We experience that peace here imperfectly, but in heaven, it will be gloriously all-encompassing.
- Phi 4:7 "And the peace of God, which passeth all understanding, shall keep your hearts and minds through Christ Jesus." To those who can't imagine how they would be able to enjoy heaven thoroughly in spite of troubling memories of earth, Paul defined the peace of God as something that goes far beyond our ability to understand.

Even here on earth there are events that take place in our lives over which we think we may go to pieces, but when we pray and plug into the peace of God, we find a reserve we didn't know we had. Even more, we find a quiet strength that comes from beyond us and that we do not begin to comprehend: it's just there and we are immersed in it. We may not be able to imagine that in heaven we will be supremely at peace about everything, but God assures us that his peace will enable us to put everything in his own perspective and be both perfectly reconciled with the past, and also gloriously engaged in the joy of our everlasting present.

God's peace is the tranquility of a heart no longer restless to find an anchor or purpose. God's peace is the satisfaction of a life focused on being involved in God's perfect plan.

God's peace is the strength to remain calm of heart in the face of threatening forces, to live by faith in the midst of temptations to doubt, to rest in our redemption and the promise of eternal life when life here is put in jeopardy.

God's peace is an attitude, a position of the mind, an assurance of the heart, a divine power, given to us by God himself for living in a world of trouble.

When we pass from this world to the next, however, this peace does not leave us. It, like everything else about our redeemed lives, will be perfected and intensified. We will have the ability to live in perfect peace about whatever has gone before. For this reason, we will simply be impervious to anxiety, regret, sorrow or grief about anything we remember about our earthly lives.

This digression on the peace of God is meant to pound persistently into our hearts the fact that in heaven nothing will disturb us. Nothing will upset us. Nothing will get the better of us. Nothing will worry us, hurt us, cause us grief, give us sorrow, stimulate regret or precipitate fear. No recollection of facts from our earthly lives will have any negative effect anymore upon our minds or hearts.

All Christians have experienced some sense of this peace from time to time. When we learn to move on after some terrible ordeal, the experience transitions from a thing that brings grief or fear to us every day, to something that causes waves of anxiety occasionally, and finally to a memory that causes us merely to soberly reflect. In heaven, we will be entirely past any negative response to these recollections.

The key to this victory over all negative emotions is the fulness of God that will characterize our lives in heaven and the age to come. Seeing things as God sees them will change our attitudes about everything. Knowing the immense satisfaction that comes from being one with God and one with Christ without exception will give us a focus on our eternal lives that will rule out any negative feeling.

Freedom, Perfection and Wholeness

More important than most other aspects of our heavenly lives will be the freedom, perfection and wholeness we anticipate experiencing. One of Paul's important inscriptions of divine revelation to him, quoted above in this chapter, is Rom 8:20-23. Look at two phrases drawn from vss.21 and 23: "the glorious liberty of the children of God" and "the redemption of our body." A third inspired description appears in Eph 4:13, "Till we all come...to a perfect man." In these three phrases are a mine of glorious expectations.

Freedom

We have already seen in the discussion above that Christians in their resurrection state will be without sin and evil and thus without causes of sorrow or any negative emotion. In fact what the new birth inaugurated will be completed when we are transferred from this realm to the heavenly realm, since we will be freed suddenly, dramatically, and totally from anything and everything that hindered us in the experience of life as God meant for us to have it.

Paul's simple phrase, "the glorious liberty of the children of God," is pregnant with the indescribable richness of the freedom we will experience in eternity. The absence of external things that provoke grief or anger is only the beginning of this liberty that will mark our living.

Human beings will continue to be creatures, of course. We will not be equal to God or be able to attain divine status, as some religions suggest; however, within the scope of our finite status, we will be able to fulfill every goal God places before us, every challenge he lays out for us, every dream he gives our glorified minds.

Our freedom will also mean there will be no limitations placed on us by doubt, no hesitations caused by fear, no barriers thrown up by difficulty, and no reluctance caused by feeble faith. We will implicitly trust God in his love and power and we will experience flawlessly the impulses he gives us.

Perfection

Not only will we be uninhibited in our pursuit of God's continuing inspiration of our lives in his eternal realm, but we will also experience perfection, the ability to be and to do everything that God, from the beginning, meant for us to become and to accomplish. This perfection is the ultimate meaning of Paul's phrase, "the redemption of our body."

From the creation narratives in Genesis, the description of the fall, and the subsequent histories of not just the Jews but of man in general, we can infer the tremendous loss in man's innate abilities and capacities that resulted from sin. The first man was able to fellowship with the Lord in a way only hinted at in scripture but which clearly involved intimacy of knowledge and feeling. Probably there were many physical attributes that were degraded or lost with the introduction of sin into God's creation. It seems obvious that but for sin, man would not have died.

God's plan of redemption in Jesus Christ was not a plan merely to save the soul but also to redeem the body. Christ's sacrifice on the cross and his resurrection from the grave bought man back from his slavery to sin and promised complete and total redemption to him—both spirit and body—if he repents and receives Christ as Saving Lord.

This bodily redemption clearly means that whatever

limitations were placed on the human body and life by sin, whatever disabilities became part of his life experience, these impediments would be finally and fully be removed when God completes the redemptive process in the event of the resurrection. Going to heaven during the present age will free the spirit to live unto God fully. Being given a resurrection body will empower the body to its perfect state within the creative purpose of God.

Wholeness

Finally, our heavenly lives, especially after the resurrection and our acquisition of our new bodies, will be distinguished by a wholeness that resembles the life of Jesus Christ himself.

Part of the challenge of our lives in the present age is dealing with the things that frustrate our desire to obey God and to be mature in every way. Our histories are pockmarked with failures that set us back and with flaws that repeatedly appear and trip us up. Our knowledge is incomplete and therefore our plans are imperfect. Our faith is often blemished and inconsistent. There are sometimes gaping holes in our emotional stability and vacuous cracks in our spirituality. We experience neediness on many levels, in our sense of purpose, our relationships, and our internal fortitude. Many of our mental, emotional and interpersonal parts are defective or broken.

Addressing this fundamental lack of wholeness or completeness, Paul wrote that the body of Christ would grow until "we all," meaning both each of us and all of us together, "come...to a perfect man." The goal of our Christian growth in this realm and the eventual glorification of every believer is to make us whole, entire, and complete. This is what Paul promised in Phi 1:6: "He which hath begun a good work in you will perform it until the day of Jesus Christ." Paul's word translated "perform" in the King James is *epiteleo,* which means specifically to bring to an end, to finish, to complete. When we move from earth to heaven, God, who has been perfecting us continually, will complete his work in us and make us entirely whole. There will be no sense of neediness anymore. We will have no emptiness in our souls, no hunger for what we cannot define, and no lack of fulfilment of any kind.

We have now seen that heaven will come to earth some day soon. Earth will be recreated in some undisclosed manner and life will be perfected in every way for the saved in Jesus Christ. We have seen also that heaven will come to earth in some spatial way. Let's take a closer look at what the Revelation to John the Apostle said specifically about how heaven and earth will meet.

6
The New Jerusalem

Many if not most Christians find reading, to say nothing of interpreting, the Book of Revelation to be a daunting task. For that reason, many believers leave Revelation out of their regular Bible reading, just as they might skip over Leviticus or any of the "begats" of scripture. They just don't think they will get much out of it.

Yet portions of Revelation are familiar fare at one of the oft recurring events of every church: funerals. At such times Christians welcome hearing the strains of Revelation 21 describing the New Jerusalem coming down out of heaven. Something about the images John saw and wrote about brings a deep and profound comfort and joyous anticipation to our hearts.

This joy is exactly what John's vision was supposed to provoke; however, knowing what the New Jerusalem was when John saw it, and what that vision may mean in actuality, is something we should inspect in greater depth. Let's look at the relevant verses from Rev 21 and, in the light of our foregoing study, come to a reasonable interpretation of what this vision given to John tells us about heaven on earth.

John's Revealing Vision

> Rev 21:10 And he carried me away in the spirit to a great and high mountain, and shewed me that great city, the holy Jerusalem, descending out of heaven

from God...

One of the seven angels, whom John had just seen with the seven last plagues, ushered John by way of vision to a mountain vantage point where he saw this "holy Jerusalem," which is the same as the "New Jerusalem" mentioned in Rev 3:12 and just a few verses ago in Rev 21:2. This holy city is not the Jerusalem of today, not the Jerusalem of Jesus' day, not even the Jerusalem of Solomon's day when the first temple was built. This is the Jerusalem of ideals, the conceptual Jerusalem, the pattern of Jerusalem, the quintessential place of life and glory and splendor. In other words, it is the epitome of heaven.

The New Jerusalem is never spoken of as fully equivalent to heaven, but certainly it typifies it. If it comes down out of heaven, it cannot be all of heaven, just as Jerusalem was not all of Judah or Israel, but it was the focal point of it.

The key to understanding this passage is interpreting this very phrase, "descending out of heaven from God." The same phrase appears in v.2. The word for descending, or coming down, is in a verb tense in Greek that means the action continues—it goes on and on. In some sense, in both Rev 21:2 and 21:10, Jerusalem was in the midst of a descent, but it did not seem to conclude that descent by finding foundations on the earth.

This particularity in John's language strongly suggests that the New Jerusalem he saw was suspended between earth and heaven and provided some sort of link, transition or portal between the two.

Hardly any purpose would seem to be served in God's giving John this vision unless it were to communicate some idea of the realities constituting heaven, especially after the events of the last days take place. While the vision may not be intended as an exact preview of heaven, the New Jerusalem, and the new earth, the depth of detail in the vision suggests that it is more than merely an ornate symbol of God's intimate dwelling with man. As vital as God's personal intimacy with man is, the imagery of Rev 21 seems intended to give us some indication of how things might look or work in the age to come.

Therefore, we are probably on firm ground in taking this vision plainly on the whole. The larger picture of scripture that involves a new heaven *and* a new earth is explained by this vision of the New Jerusalem. *It is the gateway to the throne room of God.*

Consider the city of New Jerusalem itself:

> 11 Having the glory of God: and her light was like unto a stone most precious, even like a jasper stone, clear as crystal...

First, as an overall impression, John wrote that the city manifested the presence of God in it. It was clear to John that the city as a whole was intended to reveal the glory of God. He tried to describe the quality of light that shone about the city and within it, and he could compare it only to the brilliance of gemstones, and yet not even stones that he had seen, but those that people imagined.

This process of John's seeing and then attempting to liken what he saw to earthly sights or objects is conceptually important. In the verses that follow, John repeatedly stabbed at a description and knew that he couldn't fully and accurately impart to his readers what he saw.

> 12 And had a wall great and high, and had twelve gates, and at the gates twelve angels, and names written

thereon, which are the names of the twelve tribes of the children of Israel...

The walls John saw were clearly not for protection, as the walls of all ancient cities were. Heaven needs no protection. Rather, they are visible symbols of the security of eternal life. "Gates" are more exactly gateways, for the gates are never closed (Isa 60:11).

> 13 On the east three gates; on the north three gates; on the south three gates; and on the west three gates.

The wall included gateways on all four of its sides. These would seem to represent complete access by anyone in the New Jerusalem to everything that lay on the outside of it, which would be not only all of heaven but all of the new earth and those privileged to live in it.

The details being filled in begin to give us a picture of a point of ingress and egress for both the realm of heaven and the realm of the new earth.

> 14 And the wall of the city had twelve foundations, and in them the names of the twelve apostles of the Lamb.

After the suicide of Judas, the disciples picked Matthias, one of the men who had been with them faithfully since the beginning of Jesus' ministry, to replace the traitor. Shortly, Christ called Saul of Tarsus to become Paul the Apostle. Our question of whether Matthias or Paul was to be considered the new twelfth apostle may not be answered until we reach heaven. The reference in this verse may be understood in an ideal way or we may infer our chosen candidate. The author prefers Paul.

The significance, of course, is that the twelve apostles held the same position in the New Testament church as the twelve patriarchs and tribes did in the Old Testament congregation of Israel, both sets of leaders being vital to the beginnings of their respective traditions and truths. Also we may naturally derive the truth that Christ honored his disciples for their following him when the fickle crowd came and went. They also laid down their lives for him in spreading the gospel after Pentecost and the coming of the Spirit. The New Jerusalem will no doubt actually memorialize their signal contribution to the bride of Christ.

> 15 And he that talked with me had a golden reed to measure the city, and the gates thereof, and the wall thereof.

We won't go into the details of the measurements of the city, but the numbers are representative of the completeness and immensity of God's plan, and the fullness of times in which his plan was and is completed.

> 16 And the city lieth foursquare, and the length is as large as the breadth: and he measured the city with the reed, twelve thousand furlongs. The length and the breadth and the height of it are equal.

The dimensions appear to be cubical. It is a cube of the product of the twelves of the Old Testament tribes and the New Testament apostles. Thus, it represents the fullness of the saints of the ages. We noted in a previous chapter that both Old and New Testament saints will be citizens of heaven. More broadly, this cube bounded by twelves represents the complete work of God in his creation.

> 17 And he measured the wall thereof, an hundred and forty and four cubits, according to the measure of a man, that is, of the angel.

Further featuring the number twelve, the walls were twelve times twelve cubits thick, about 216 feet or about 66 meters. Again, there will be no reason for the walls of a heavenly city even to exist, much less to be so thick. The heftiness of an ancient city's wall was for one reason, namely safety. No danger appears to threaten the New Jerusalem. These walls seem to be purely for definition. The New Jerusalem is no indefinite, sprawling area like Jacksonville, Florida, or Los Angeles, California, where one hardly knows if he has left the city proper and gone into some other incorporated area. This heavenly city is demarcated by its walls, which themselves are full of symbolic meaning and, not inconsequentially, great beauty:

> 18 And the building of the wall of it was of jasper: and the city was pure gold, like unto clear glass.

Ancient jasper was probably opaque, but something about the composition of the wall John saw reminded him of both jasper and clear glass (v.11).

The composition of the city's buildings or structures looked like gold to John, but also like glass. He left the description at that.

> 19 And the foundations of the wall of the city were garnished with all manner of precious stones. The first foundation was jasper; the second, sapphire; the third,

a chalcedony; the fourth, an emerald; 20 The fifth, sardonyx; the sixth, sardius; the seventh, chrysolite; the eighth, beryl; the ninth, a topaz; the tenth, a chrysoprasus; the eleventh, a jacinth; the twelfth, an amethyst. 21 And the twelve gates were twelve pearls; every several gate was of one pearl: and the street of the city was pure gold, as it were transparent glass.

There are many focused studies on the possible meanings of the individual stones John identified or attempted to describe in the walls of the New Jerusalem. Some suggest that the stones are messages to the church in this age, representing the work of Christ in salvation, the ministry of the Spirit, and the traits the Christian should have. Others find the full range of key theological principles in the whole Bible. Still others think the stones stand for principles for living that constitute the way to heaven. Much similarity exists between these interpretations.

The scope of our study does not require our picking an existing interpretation or devising a new one. Suffice it to say that the image of the walls of the New Jerusalem leaves no doubt that God knows how to decorate!

As well, our rather simple summation that heaven has streets of gold falls short, in fact, of a proper assessment. Again, John combines contradictory terms for what he saw, which in itself suggests that what he saw was beyond full, human comprehension. Gold is not clear, but the gold of these heavenly streets was clear like glass as well as being golden—like gold!

The interpretation of many people focuses on the opulence and the precious value of heaven's construction materials, as if the deprived of earth will finally have their share of gold and jewels when they get to heaven. Many people, however, are not impressed with gold and jewels in this life. They value other things more. Will they be disappointed with heaven, or think that it's gaudy?

Clearly there is some other point to the luxurious, palatial beauty of the New Jerusalem. The overall picture seems to communicate several things to us:

- The most precious and valuable substances in the heavenly universe are appropriate as building materials for the place where God uniquely displays his glorious presence.
- The value and permanence of heaven's substance far exceed anything we have valued or amassed on earth.
- All people appreciate things of beauty and will find God's dwelling place to be of unsurpassed exquisiteness.

It is also worth repeating our observation that the New Jerusalem will not be the entirety of heaven, and that the entire universe will exist besides, as the domain of the redeemed. The glistening city where God's throne room is, is one location only, in an infinite place made for God's people.

22 And I saw no temple therein: for the Lord God Almighty and the Lamb are the temple of it.

The similar vision of the prophet Ezekiel featured a temple. It represented the restoration of the worship of God in a restored Israel. Some believe it was intended to be a blueprint for Israel's rebuilding of the temple, which could not have happened until after 1948 in any event, but which is rumored to be on the drawing board in our times.

John by contrast *did not* see a temple, and he understood implicitly that there was no need of a building designated to be a temple, since God himself was the place of worship and the Lamb of God, the Eternal Son, was the One in whom all heaven's residents would worship God.

The matter of the temple is a digression we will not pursue except to say that other references in Revelation to the presence of a temple (3:12, 7:15, 11:1, 11:19, 14:15, 14:17, 15:5, 15:6, 15:8, 16:1, and 16:17) refer either to the presence of God himself or else to earth before its remaking. Some likeness of a temple on earth seems to be referred to during the tribulation.

> 23 And the city had no need of the sun, neither of the moon, to shine in it: for the glory of God did lighten it, and the Lamb is the light thereof.

Some interpreters, especially those who do not incorporate an entire universe in their concept of the new earth and heaven, think that the earth will have no sun anymore. This is not what John saw or described. Let us remember that he is describing the New Jerusalem only, which is not even all of heaven but only one part of it. It is "the city" that had "no need of the sun." Light for the city comes from the presence of the triune God within it in a glorious way. As we said in Chapter 3, God has given himself a locale, a specific place of his making, where his glory is exhibited in a special way, apparently for the benefit of all created beings. The New Jerusalem appears to be his throne room where his personal glory is manifested in the form of visible light. This interesting fact is alluded to again in 21:25 and 22:1, both of which refer to the New Jerusalem or the entire heavenly realm, rather than the new earth or any of the physical universe.

The city of the New Jerusalem will indeed never sleep. It

will be lit all the time. Its purpose is not served by its being dark when earth or any other planet is experiencing night. We will look at the purpose of the New Jerusalem shortly.

> 24 And the nations of them which are saved shall walk in the light of it: and the kings of the earth do bring their glory and honour into it.

There has been much discussion among commentators about "nations" in this verse. Some think it refers to the Gentiles (a common translation of the Greek word) and refers to universal salvation. Others say these nations are earthly powers who belong to God and enter heaven at last, bringing their earthly splendor. These views fail to consider the new order of *earth and heaven*.

In what we might call the "cosmology" of the future after the resurrection, if one conceived of only a heaven and nothing else, no earth or universe, this verse would pose a confusing problem. If one conceived of heaven as merely a spiritual place of bright lights and worship, this verse would still be a problem. However, with a "cosmology" featuring a heavenly realm, a city with the throne of God, and a new earth in its infinite universe, no problem remains.

It appears from coordinating this and other verses in Revelation that this view is correct. The "nations" would be the peoples—all redeemed—who populate the new earth and have access to the heavenly city, and to the very presence of God. They are pictured as bringing splendor, i.e., offerings of beauty, into the place where God is worshiped. It would seem that such pilgrimages with offerings take place repeatedly or even continually.

As a side note, we should be reminded that in John's day there was little that would constitute astronomy as a body of knowledge. Our solar system was not understood as comprising orbiting bodies all hanging in space. No one understood that the earth was actually 93 million miles from the sun or that Saturn was 886 million miles from it. People in John's day didn't have any idea that our sun is part of a galaxy of billions of suns, much less that our galaxy is only one of millions or billions of such galaxies in a nearly infinite universe. When Peter said we look for a new heavens and a new earth, he was of course referring to this earth and probably to the visible heavens or merely the sky relative to this earth. When John spoke of people on the new earth as recorded in Rev 21:24 he was not suggesting that the rest of the universe experienced any cataclysmic cleansing or reformation, since he almost certainly didn't have knowledge of worlds beyond this earth.

Indeed, it is reasonable for us to conclude that sin is a spiritual disease particular to the earth and the human beings who live and have lived upon it. What fiery destruction and re-creation God plans as closure to this present, sinful age is likely restricted to this earth proper, with the rest of the universe left intact.

> 25 And the gates of it shall not be shut at all by day: for there shall be no night there.

As we previously implied, gates were shut at night for protection and opened in the day for commerce and travel. Open gates again imply entrance and egress. Though exiting the city is not mentioned, if it were not allowed or possible to do so, there would be no gates, or the scripture would likely say that after everybody entered, the gates were sealed shut. To the contrary, this verse implies going in and out.

26 And they shall bring the glory and honour of the nations into it. 27 And there shall in no wise enter into it any thing that defileth, neither whatsoever worketh abomination, or maketh a lie: but they which are written in the Lamb's book of life.

If there *were* any such beings who were evil, they would be refused entrance. The continual openness of the gates indicates that such people no longer exist, certainly not in the new earth, and such corrupt practices are not to be found.

John's vision of the holy city, the ancient prophets' visions of heaven, Peter's prophecies and Paul's teachings present us with varied information offered to meet different needs. It is possible, however, to piece together the strains of what the Bible authors have told us and to identify the places and the strata, so to speak, of the heavenly life to come.

Heaven's Geography

Revelation's record of John's vision of the New Jerusalem, the many references throughout the Old and New Testaments concerning heaven, and the prophecies of judgment, destruction and the re-creation of the world, lead us to a conclusion that is imminently defensible from scripture and reasonable deductions. The Heavenly City of New Jerusalem, anything else described as heaven, and the new earth, are all part of *Heaven* as a single term for eternal life to come. When the Bible refers to heaven as a place or a life after the end of this age, the term incorporates all we have learned of the heaven of heavens, the New Jerusalem, and the re-created earth and the rest of the universe.

The Throne Room Where We Worship

The New Jerusalem contains the throne room of God (Rev 22:3). As discussed, this is the place God chooses to specially make his glory known in a personal way. Consequently, it is where the most pointed, intensified, focused worship of God will take place. The author of Hebrews had this throne room in mind when he wrote:

> But ye are come unto mount Sion, and unto the city of the living God, the heavenly Jerusalem, and to an innumerable company of angels, to the general assembly and church of the firstborn, which are written in heaven, and to God the Judge of all, and to the spirits of just men made perfect... (Heb 12:22-23).

These two verses identify the New Jerusalem in heaven and the throne of God in New Jerusalem, just as John's vision did. There in the presence of God are the angels and the glorified redeemed of the earth. The context is worship.

Essentially, we will go to church in the throne room of the heavenly city. This will be the place where we will gather for definitive worship of God.

The City Where We Commune with Jesus

From the dimensions given in Rev 21:16, the New Jerusalem, which again seems to be cubical, is more than 1,400 miles on a side, making it a truly immense place. From Washington, D.C., to the other side of the Rocky Mountains in Colorado to the west, is about 1,400 miles. Within this gigantic heavenly city, other than the throne room of God there would appear to be many other sights and places, possibly all the dwellings Jesus spoke of in Joh 14:2. It would also seem to be the location of heavenly communion with the

Lord Jesus.

Being with Jesus in heaven. Jesus himself indicated that when the new age of the kingdom was fully come—after the end of this present age—people would be able to commune with God, and as Jesus implied, with him:

> And they shall come from the east, and from the west, and from the north, and from the south, and shall sit down in the kingdom of God (Luk 13:29).

Rev 22:1,3, etc. locate the enthroned Jesus in the heavenly city, so the feast Jesus spoke of will take place in the New Jerusalem. Communion with him personally and bodily will take place there as well. Note that Jesus' description of people coming from all directions indicates travel. They will gather to be with Jesus. The feast will be continuous, and trips to the holy city for feasting/fellowship with Christ will be continual.

One of the more glorious facts about heavenly life is that God the Son, who before the incarnation was not bodily at all, will in the heavenly city be visible as the resurrected and ascended Christ.

The eternal Son became a human being at his conception in Nazareth and was born a baby in Bethlehem. He was crucified as a man on Calvary outside Jerusalem and entombed nearby. The third day after, he rose as the firstfruits of the resurrection that awaits all of us who are redeemed through him. Forty days after that, he went from earth to heaven in view of his disciples. According to the prayer of Jesus recorded in John's gospel, Jesus was to reacquire the glory he had with the Father before the world existed (Joh 17:5). However, John later wrote that the ascended Jesus kept his resurrection body when he returned to the Father:

> Beloved, now are we the sons of God, and it doth not yet appear what we shall be: but we know that, when he shall appear, we shall be like him; for we shall see him as he is (1Jo 3:2).

The language and logic of this verse are very clear. Since the ascension, Jesus has existed in his resurrected form, a continuing memorial to his own redemptive work and to the divine condescension to man that made possible our coming back into fellowship with God. That we who are saved will eventually be like our Savior proves that he has his resurrection body in heaven, since we could not be like him in his omnipresent state.

This astounding fact, that Jesus in heaven is in bodily form, speaks of the unparalleled sacrifice he made and the almost incredible alteration he was willing to make in order to save sinners. He became something he had not been in order to redeem us, and the change became permanent, though in a resurrection body of glorious differences that we have only an inkling of now.

For those who think of the technical ramifications of Jesus' bodily form and wonder how any and all of us who wish to spend time with him personally would ever have a chance to do so, we need only recall that after the resurrection in Jerusalem, Jesus appeared at will to his disciples and to others, without needing to travel and without any limitations, spatially, temporally or otherwise. It would seem that in his unique resurrection body, his omnipresence and his specific location in a body are not mutually exclusive.

This observation suggests that no one's desire to be with Jesus will be frustrated by his being with someone else at the same time.

Experiencing perfect health and sustenance. Also shown in the New Jerusalem, the heavenly city, are the water and tree of life:

> And he shewed me a pure river of water of life, clear as crystal, proceeding out of the throne of God and of the Lamb. In the midst of the street of it, and on either side of the river, was there the tree of life, which bare twelve manner of fruits, and yielded her fruit every month: and the leaves of the tree were for the healing of the nations (Rev 22:1-2).

Extensive treatments have been developed on these features of the heavenly city. We will not attempt to survey those studies, but the water of life, the tree of life and the healing leaves appear to be, like the walls of heaven, visible symbols of permanent and perpetual realities for all heaven's citizens. The fact that revelation gives no picture of anyone repeatedly drinking from the river, eating the food, or applying the leaves, suggests strongly that these things are symbols. If there were diseases requiring the leaves actually to be used, that fact would contradict other evidence for the perfections of the heavenly life.

Living in many "mansions." Finally, as we suggested earlier in this chapter, the New Jerusalem may be the site of the "many mansions" Jesus told his disciples he was going to heaven to prepare for them. The Greek word translated "mansions" in the KJV means "dwellings," not necessarily the palatial estates we think of when we hear the word in English today.

It is perhaps false modesty for someone to ask the Lord apologetically to build him a little cabin in a corner of heaven. It would be equally as indicative of sinful pride to ask God to prepare the heavenly equivalent of the Biltmore House.

Doubtless God knows what kind of dwellings we will need or want, and who is to say that the size, configuration or design of those dwellings may not change from time to time in the realm where time means nothing?

The Land Where We Dwell Forever

The heaven where God and the angels are includes the holy city, the New Jerusalem, which we have seen is in a state of continual descent out of heaven. Its ingress and egress, emphasized by its always-open gateways, imply the transit of heaven's citizens between heaven proper and the new earth. This new earth, re-created from the earth that will fall under the cataclysmic judgment of God in the end times, and the rest of the universe God made in the beginning, constitute the land where we, the redeemed of God, will dwell forever.

An interesting description appears in Rev 22:15, where John wrote that "For without are dogs, and sorcerers, and whoremongers, and murderers, and idolaters, and whosoever loveth and maketh a lie." Verse 14 had just mentioned the city (New Jerusalem) and had spoken of those privileged to enter into it. From these two verses alone, if pulled out of their whole-Bible context, it might appear that anywhere outside of the New Jerusalem one might expect to find evildoers lurking.

It would be a mistake to take v.15 so restrictively. First, too many verses in the rest of Revelation, to say nothing of the rest of the Bible, mention the new earth and the re-created natural order as accessible to the redeemed. Second, John has already described New Jerusalem as coming down out of heaven, such that it is not the entirety of heaven. The rest of heaven is certainly not populated by evildoers. Third, If heaven were restricted to the New Jerusalem, then a cube a mere 1,400 miles on a side would constitute God's abode, and the rest of the universe, as well as anything that exists otherwise, would be relegated to evildoers and, one might reasonably conclude, Satan. Clearly this would be the reverse of what one would rightly expect. Surely God, his angels and all of his saints are not "holed up" in a cube while Satan and the hordes of hell take over the rest of the universe.

Rather, "outside" must refer to whatever lies outside of the three strata of the heavenly life: heaven, new earth, and New Jerusalem as the portal between the two. This one verse must be viewed in light of the many other statements and implications that view the vistas of heavenly life to be expansive and the prospects of hell by contrast to be confined.

One could use the example of any ancient city controlling a country, such as Jerusalem itself. The city would include the palace of the king and the place of worship. The walls would encompass a much wider area and take in many citizens living under the protective rule of the king. However, the land lying outside the city, for miles and miles around, would also be under the king's rule and protection, to the extent of the country's borders. In an imperfect world like ours, both the city and the countryside outside it would have their share of criminals. In a perfect world, there would be no one within the sphere of the king's domain, inside the city or outside, who would do evil.

Similarly, the New Jerusalem is a metaphor for all of the heavenly life, which includes both heaven and the new earth. The "dogs" and other evil persons are *completely outside*, i.e., in outer darkness, from which God will have withdrawn his presence forever.

The new earth, which includes our planet and the rest of the universe in which we live, will be the land where we, God's people, dwell forever. It will be our place of adventure, discovery, accomplishment and yes, play. Some interpreters have suggested that as many planets as probably exist in the universe, there would be enough for every citizen of heaven to have one. Others surmise that having the ability to transport ourselves to any place in the heavenly domain, we may choose to go to distant planets and not only see their new beauties but also develop places to stay for long periods of time. No hard evidence in the Bible gives us any basis for more than informed speculation.

So far our study indicates that the vista of heavenly life will take in the immensity of the physical universe as well as the heavenly one, with the portal city of the New Jerusalem constituting the center of worship and fellowship with God. This concept, however, may be unfamiliar or even startling to many people. Let us address the possible disparity between our findings on heaven and the ideas others may have about what to expect on the other side of this life.

7
HEAVEN, GOD'S VICTORY

Most Christians in the world do not have a scholar's grasp of the teachings of Revelation or an extensive knowledge of Bible prophecy. Many Christians do not have a detailed familiarity with systematic theology. Frankly, many if not most Christians leave it to their ministers and seminary professors to deal with these doctrinal issues.

Similarly, many if not most Christians have a very basic view of heaven that doesn't include many details. They may anticipate that heaven will be a bright, airy place where they will see loved ones, walk on streets of gold, go to see Jesus, and perhaps spend most of their time before the throne of God singing praises along with the angels and a vast congregation of Christians. They may not have thought about there being much more to heaven than this.

The introduction of ideas such as those contained in this book may already have caused a reader to respond quizzically or with skepticism. This study is an interpretation of the Bible's teachings about an expansive heaven and varied heavenly life; however, even though our interpretation is based on specific Bible passages, readers who are new to these concepts may have doubts simply because these views differ from what they have always believed.

Causes of Skepticism

Various causes exist for skepticism about a more detailed

view of what we can expect about heavenly life.

Prejudiced by Acquired Beliefs

Perhaps the most prevalent reason for skepticism is the fact that many people are prejudiced by acquired beliefs.

We aren't supposed to know. Some Christians relegate a great deal of the Bible to a body of mysteries about which they say summarily, 'We aren't meant to understand everything in the Bible.' Surprisingly, the entire book of Revelation often goes into this category. During the course of his church ministry years, this author heard dozens of people offer that opinion about John's apocalyptic writing. Yet the book of Revelation itself offers this challenge: "Blessed is he that readeth, and they that hear the words of this prophecy, and keep those things which are written therein: for the time is at hand" (Rev 1:3). Apparently, neither John nor Christ, who gave him the apocalypse, thought that interpreting Revelation is impossible. At most, it is difficult. Perhaps the difficulty is what makes most Christians avoid it, and then they rationalize their avoidance by suggesting that it can't be understood anyway.

I've always heard. Another reason for initial reluctance to accept a different view of heaven is simply the fact that many people have always heard that heaven is this thing or that, and any new idea challenges what they believed was common knowledge. Many non-Christians have always heard that heaven was fluffy clouds and white robes and wings and people playing harps. On that basis, they may actually lampoon Christians' belief in heaven. Even many Christians don't have a much more sophisticated view of heaven, simply because they've merely adopted what they've heard, without investigating what the Bible actually says.

People can't always explain where they got their views, but

most of us tend to be certain of what we've always assumed was so. It is for that reason, by the way, that many a destructive prejudice prevails in the world: people don't allow their beliefs to be challenged. Simplistic or errant Bible interpretations can also be destructive, or at least counter-productive to Christian growth, gospel witness, and faith-building.

People who have seen heaven and come back. Some people have modified or confirmed their beliefs about heaven after hearing or reading about someone who claimed to have gone to heaven and come back. At the time of this writing, a highly publicized account is making the rounds about a young boy who says he had such an experience. Such NDEs, as we discussed previously in this book, should always be evaluated in the light of scripture, but unfortunately, many people take these reports at face value and do not compare them to what the Bible says. Even worse, many people value contemporary experience over scriptural revelation in the first place. Beliefs shaped in this way are difficult to reconcile with clear exposition of the Bible.

Misled by Mistaken Theology

While many people bring cultural prejudices and other non-scriptural sources to their beliefs about heaven, sadly many others derive their views from Christian sources.

My preacher said. Ideally we should be able to come to a solid, biblical understanding of spiritual concepts by faithfully listening to our preachers and teachers in church. In the real world, many preachers are untrained or under-trained and are not good expositors of the scriptures. Many of them bring their own, poorly-founded prejudices into their ministries and preach them from the pulpit.

While writing this very portion of this book, the author

took in a Bible study where a retired pastor led the hour's gathering. At least a dozen times in the course of a rambling presentation of a topical "study," this older gentleman said, "Now, what I'm going to tell you may be true, I don't know, but I believe it..." followed by a statement of dubious opinion or of generic spirituality not supported by any specific scriptural authority. If this was the minister's pattern of preaching during his fifty-plus year ministry, no doubt many people in his congregation who relied on him alone for their beliefs acquired some ideas that had little basis in God's written record of his self-revelation—the Bible.

Our study, by contrast, has been based on the teachings of the scripture, as we have compared scripture with scripture and tried to remain true to the discernable purposes of the authors and the evidence of the original languages.

I read a book once. Some Christians do attempt to study the great mysteries of the Bible, and their study method may include heavy reliance on books other than the Bible. Obviously, there are many good books on the Bible or subjects in the Bible written by reputable authors—This author hopes this book will be one of them! Many people, however, may be indiscriminate about their choice of authors or uninformed about scholarly issues that render some books highly questionable.

I heard on Christian radio or TV. Not only are many books not worthwhile sources of authoritative information, television and radio—even those stations purporting to be Christian in content—may feature teachers, preachers or interviewees whose views about heaven are an unreliable mix of scriptural fact and cultural fiction.

Inadequate personal study. Perhaps the bottom line is that Christians often don't take upon themselves the responsibility of studying the Bible for themselves, using reliable materials and spending sufficient time to develop mature and biblically defensible interpretations. We in the Protestant tradition value our reliance on the Bible, but we also value our reliance on ourselves, not any requisite human intermediary, to study and know the Bible. We call this the Priesthood of the Believer. We believe we cannot only read the Bible for ourselves but also understand it with the aid of the Holy Spirit. Unfortunately, while we may preach this firmly, we often don't take the time to practice it very faithfully. Inadequate personal study of God's word results in much of our mistaken information.

Reasons for Revising Our Beliefs

If we need more than a simple study of the subject-specific scriptures themselves to convince us of Bible truths about heaven, perhaps some general arguments from the wider context of the Bible will help us put the matter in perspective.

God's Original Plan for Creation

The heaven we have discovered in the course of this study so far is one that includes the universe we have come to know as virtually infinite and filled with billions of galaxies, each with billions of stars like our sun. By contrast, some simplistic views of our eternal future involve the destruction of our universe. In such interpretations, God simply scraps what he created and substitutes an aery place with no particular landscape as our heavenly confines—sorry: our heavenly home, forever.

To the contrary, the concept that can be derived inductively from the Bible is that God's original plan for creation was that man exist in a vast universe of space, time and astronomical richness and beauty that still defies us to comprehend. What passage of scripture ever suggests that God has or ever will give up on his original plan for creation?

We have looked briefly in this study at prophecies of God's re-creating or refurbishing his created works, such that in the earth, in particular, the animal kingdom reverts to his nonviolent plan. Peter's prophecy adds the general assertion that we look for a new heavens and new earth. Paul's teaching was that the creation itself groaned while it waited to be redeemed from the effects of man's sin.

These specific passages, interpreted in the light of God's redemptive activity throughout his people's history, suggest almost beyond contradiction that God will not scrap his original plans. He will merely cleanse his creation of everything that brought destruction and ruin into it.

In that creation, man walked in the garden with the Lord. There was no death. Man was given dominion over the earth. In the new creation, man will walk in the heavenly city and by its river of life with the Lord. There will be no death anymore. Man will continue to have dominion over the universe of worlds like ours. This is God's original plan, perhaps multiplied and expanded, but not a whit diminished by the hour of judgment to come.

God's Intent to Win

God's original plan will be continued because God's intent is to be victorious over the forces of evil. God created the angel who made himself the devil. Certainly God knew this would happen. (Why, is for another book!) The Bible is the story of God's intentions and his activities designed to defeat Satan on the territory that Satan thought to mark out for himself—earth.

Can anyone read the Bible and come away with an idea that Satan will win? The lesson is drawn repeatedly from holy history that God defeats evil, if for no other reason than that Satan is not a god. He could be destroyed by a simple word from God. God's quest, however, is to woo his creature, man, to himself by choice, and then to destroy evil at the end and exclude from his presence those who doggedly choose to stick with the one who led them astray and kept them prisoners. The 20th chapter of Revelation is high drama bearing the message that God will win.

In light of the certainty that God will win, is there any biblical basis for believing that God will concede a partial victory to Satan? There isn't. And since there isn't, there is no scriptural basis for believing that life after this life will somehow be less interesting, less varied, less spacious, less qualitative, less fulfilling, less exciting, than this life is now. Our interpretation so far has raised the prospect of many activities, discoveries and experiences that "blow the lid off" much of the prevailing cultural idea of heaven.

Consider as final arguments the convictions of two Old Testament authors:

> I know that You can do anything and no plan of Yours can be thwarted (Job 42:2 HCSB).

> The Lord frustrates the counsel of the nations; He thwarts the plans of the peoples (Psa 33:10 HCSB).

God does not intend to be thwarted. Instead, he frustrates the purposes of sin and sinners, and the father of sinners, Satan. Heaven will be a grand demonstration of God's victory, on a universal scale.

8
Our Lives in Heaven

Knowing there is a heaven for God's redeemed people leads us to a lively curiosity about what heaven will be like. The Bible gives us little clues here and there that suggest various qualities about heavenly life. We already know from our study that the triune God makes himself known specially in heaven, that angels will be there, and that we may expect the fellowship and company of all the saints of the ages past and future. We know something of the "geography" of the sphere of heavenly places, that it will include the heaven of heavens, the New Jerusalem, and the re-created earth in the universe.

What, however, will our own lives be like? Consider several fascinating glimpses into our heavenly existence.

Bodily but Not Sexual

Jesus revealed an important fact about human lives in the life to come, when he answered a question posed by some Sadducees. This liberal Jewish group did not believe in the resurrection of the dead to come, and they devised what they thought was a conundrum that would stump Jesus and force him to acknowledge, if only tacitly, that the resurrection didn't make sense. They proposed the case of a woman who was married to seven brothers (according to Levirite law), one after the other. She and they all died. The question to Jesus was, which one would she be married to after the resurrection, or "in the resurrection" life? Here was Jesus' reply:

> "...The children of this world marry, and are given in marriage: But they which shall be accounted worthy to obtain that world, and the resurrection from the dead, neither marry, nor are given in marriage: Neither can they die any more: for they are equal unto the angels; and are the children of God, being the children of the resurrection" (Luk 20:34-36).

Matthew's account is similar:

> "For in the resurrection they neither marry, nor are given in marriage, but are as the angels of God in heaven" (Mat 22:30).

Jesus went on to make a succinct case for the resurrection, but his remarks about marriage, angels, and resurrected human beings are wonderfully revealing on a subject about which many of us have questions.

Marriage, Sex, and Procreation

First, Jesus' statement that "in the resurrection" human beings will be "as the angels" (Mat) or "equal unto the angels" (Luk), must be taken in the context of the specific subject of marriage, not as a general description of what people will become. Jesus was saying that the factors that necessitate marriage or that marriage involves in the present time will no longer be factors in heaven. He was also saying that at the present time, the angels do not have those factors involved in their existence. What are those factors?

Essentially, Jesus was talking about sexual intercourse and

procreation, which according to God's standards take place permissibly and righteously only within the bond of marriage. Whatever change takes place in us upon the receipt of our resurrection bodies, we will no longer need marriage, no longer participate in marriage, no longer express ourselves through sexual union, and no longer procreate. In these respects, we will resemble the angels, whose lives in God's presence do not include these traits of human life on earth.

People who can't imagine being non-sexual or who resist the idea of leaving behind a pleasurable aspect of human life may simply be revealing their attraction to the flesh as opposed to their affinity for the spirit. To place the absence of sexuality into proper perspective, it is worth pondering the fact that any number of human activities may become superfluous or may be eliminated in the heavenly life. Almost certainly there will be no commerce and no money. People who live for money now would not welcome the prospect of a world without it—and to be sure, most people who live for money here will not be among the number who go to heaven in the first place! They will have chosen money over Christ.

Christians who love hunting will not be able to pursue it in the heavenly life, even in the new earth. However, any hunter can conceive of the pure joy of being able to walk up to a fine, ten-point buck and stroke his flanks, and sense a communion of living beings with each other that rarely takes place here. The exchange of an earthly pleasure for a surpassing heavenly joy will be totally satisfying.

The absence of marriage and, as Jesus was clearly saying, the absence of sexual relations in heaven, clearly leads us to conclude two corollary facts:

Earthly marriages will not continue. As sweet as it sounds for husbands and wives to place on their gravestones, "Forever together," the fact is that when we become citizens of heaven our earthly marriages will not transfer with us. The marriage relationship will simply not be relevant to heavenly life.

Nothing about this fact suggests that married couples who loved each other dearly will love each other any less. The love will continue, but it will not be tied to any covenant relationship or domestic obligations. As wonderful as a married couple's love may be now, the love of each will be even more profound and will rise above the physical needs and mutual responsibility that were involved in human marriage.

If couples who can't imagine not being married are reluctant to believe that heaven will not include marriage, consider those couples who feel the other way. Even some Christians who are married, for all their individual wishing that their relationship was better, warmer, closer, or more spiritual, would not want their marriage to go on in heaven. If it were God's plan for marriage to continue, then of course when all sin were removed from men and women, marriages that were blase or even full of troubles would instantly improve to the point of perfection. However, marriage will simply not exist anymore in heaven. The clear words of Jesus cannot be watered down.

No children will be born. Since there will be no sexual relations, there will be no procreation. No more children will be born.

The author would be among those who would find this fact to be a mystery. Children can be such a joy here on earth. They can also be sources of irritation, trial and even heartbreak—but isn't that true of adults?! To have no children running around heaven, though, seems mysterious, especially in the light of Jesus' assertion that "of such is the kingdom of heaven" (Mat 19:14).

One cannot conceive of a heavenly life, however, in which

marriage would not exist but sexual intercourse would continue and children would be procreated from those casual unions. Someone might propose that sex could continue but for no other purpose than sex, rather like having eternal birth control. This theory would be an obvious attempt to accommodate an earthly preoccupation with sexual pleasure. We could not conceive, however, of God, who assigned sexual union to the confines of marriage, putting that matter topsy turvy and making sex permissible between anybody and everybody in heaven, just because some human beings now can't imagine living without it.

People who have achieved deep, rich friendships here within a marriage understand that the bodily experience of sexual union, while enjoyable, is fleeting and even ephemeral. Mature people have already begun to develop the ability to conceive of a life that rises above and goes beyond the pleasures of this life. Whatever we may think now that we'll miss in heaven, we will gain so much more that we will never think of those things again.

As an illustration, consider Jesus' meeting with the woman at the well. He spent the afternoon telling her about spiritual things while his disciples were off in town buying food. When she left and the disciples came back they wanted him to eat. Jesus told them, "I have meat to eat that ye know not of" (Joh 4:32). He was so wrapped up in more important things that he had not given physical hunger any thought, and remained in that mood apparently for a while.

Probably any of us can add to that story our own experiences in being deeply involved in some project or engrossed in some greatly entertaining activity and realizing only later that we were hours past meal time.

Eating is one of our favorite pleasures in this life. But we can forget about it for a time when something more important or more exciting captures our attention. Heaven will be like that *permanently* for all the things we think we couldn't live without here on earth. They will simply be absent from heavenly life because of our new natures. We won't need or desire to do things that aren't part of our new natures anymore.

Gender may well continue. In spite of the fact that marriage and sex will not be part of our heavenly lives, gender may well be. Having sex does not define our humanity, but the case is not the same with having or being a gender. Human gender is about much more than sexual functions. We understand that what makes men men and women women is more deeply involved in their outlook on life, their style of relationships and other things. It is possible that gender identification will continue in some fashion in heaven.

There is no scripture directly suggesting that people will be unisex in heaven. Jesus' comments about our being "as the angels" related to marriage and sex, but it would be a mistake to argue, at least on the basis of that passage of scripture, that he was saying there would be no men or women, only genderless persons. If we made such an argument, we would have to then contend with the fact that in the Bible, angels, when described, are all pictured as men. The angels by the open tomb were men. The names of angels—Michael, Gabriel, etc.—are men's names. While we have no accounts of women angels (raising the interesting question of where we get the idea that angels are beautiful, blonde women), the fact that those we do have accounts of are associated with the male gender, certainly suggests that in their visible form in earth, angels looked like one gender or the other.

Nevertheless, we should be careful about concluding with absolute certainty that men will continue to be men and women to be women. As far as the evidence is concerned, the case is not closed on the issue. God knows, of course, but we ourselves cannot say for certain.

It would be difficult to speculate further on the matter of gender. For instance, if gender continued to identify us, what would our physiology be? Would our bodies be distinctively male or female?

The only solid indication of our physiology if gender were to be retained, would be an inference drawn from Jesus' comparison of us to the angels as to the matter of marriage and sex. We will not need sexual features if our lives will not feature sex. Other than this possible evidence, in the absence of a definitive answer to whether or not gender will continue, we simply cannot speculate on any subsidiary question.

What we can say is that as important as our gender and sexuality may seem to us now, we can rest assured that when we translate from earthly to heavenly bodies, what we become will be absolutely welcome to us. What we leave behind will not be missed. Remember that there will be no sorrow in heaven!

Unchanged for Eternity

In Luke's account of Jesus' answer to the Sadducees he said of those "accounted worthy to obtain that world [heaven]" that "neither can they die anymore" (Luk 20:36). The Greek words for eternal life, *aionios zoe,* mean exactly that: of indeterminate duration, everlasting, never-ending life. People in heaven will never die. Life will go on and on and on.

It is part and parcel of such an idea that we will never age. Aging is part of this life, where we eventually die. The heavenly life knows no such aging, breaking down, disease or dying.

Some people propose that life will be eternal because there will be no such thing as time. This is an idea based on a mistaken assumption about time, and possibly because of an errant reading of scripture.

Sometimes 2Pe 3:8 is adduced as proof of this opinion. There Peter stated that "one day is with the Lord as a thousand years, and a thousand years as one day." He noted this proverbial wisdom as a means of correcting people who were impatient for the Lord to return or who had concluded that because it had been twenty years or so since the ascension of Christ, he must not be coming back. Peter wanted them to realize that God's timing was quite different, and that in fact God was not distracted by long passages of time. God, who is by nature eternal, doesn't lose track or forget, as we might because of the passage of time.

Peter was not saying that in heaven there is no time. He wasn't addressing that issue at all. Neither can we jump to the conclusion that because our lives will be never ending in heaven, therefore there will be no time.

Physicists tell us that time is a function of matter and space, that the expansion of space and the formation of matter from energy involve time as a basic component. Einstein's famous equation, $E=MC^2$, expresses the relationship of time to matter, because the C in the equation stands for Constant, and the Constant is the speed of light, approximately 186,282 miles per second. Even if we don't understand the physics of time, however, we all realize that time is the measure of the passing of events. When you read this sentence, you have taken *time* to do so. If there were no time, there would be no events. Events by definition *take time*, at least for everything finite, like we are.

Even if in the heaven of heavens we are in some different dimension or universe, we will have some equivalent of time, because the scriptures say we will *do* things there. We will worship. We will gather. We will feast with Christ. We will go in and out of the heavenly city. When we go out, we will pass the time it took to leave where we were when we were inside. The basic idea of time is simply that we are able to move from here to there, do this or that, begin and finish something. Time is a function of any event, and our lives in heaven will consist of many wonderful events!

The difference in heaven will not be that there *is* no time, but that time will *mean* very little, because there will be no end to it. We will never run out of time to do things.

Because we will never die, it seems an obvious conclusion that we will not change. At least, we may say that we will not change because of the passage of heavenly time. This is not to say that we may not have the ability to change ourselves. In his resurrection body, Jesus was able to make himself unrecognizable to the group he met on the road to Emmaus. Possibly when Mary failed to recognize Jesus at the garden tomb it was because Jesus changed his appearance momentarily. These passages may imply that in our resurrection bodies, which will be like that of Jesus, we will have similar abilities. We will not change, however, by any inescapable process associated with aging, since we will not grow old.

On the basis of the fact that we will not age or die, people sometimes wonder what "age" we will be. Will we appear to be sixteen? Twenty-one? Thirty? Our concepts of an ideal age differ with our own ages now or other emotional factors. The author's mother once had a dream she believed was a vision, in which she saw her father on the other side of a bright, heaven-like street. He waved at her and signaled to her that he was happy. She said he appeared to be about forty.

Probably the best answer to the question is that we will be

no age in particular but will be recognizable to each other as who we are ideally. Christian children who die at ten or fifteen will not appear to be children, in all likelihood. They will also have an ideal appearance. This concept would seem to make the most sense in view of the scant evidence we have. (The possibility exists, of course, that we may all have the ability to change our appearance to that of children or people of any age, for whatever reason.)

Like Jesus

No higher, greater or more comprehensive description of what our lives will be like in heaven can be given than to say that we will be like Jesus:

> " Beloved, now are we the sons of God, and it doth not yet appear what we shall be: but we know that, when he shall appear, we shall be like him; for we shall see him as he is" (1Jo 3:2).

> "For our conversation is in heaven; from whence also we look for the Saviour, the Lord Jesus Christ: Who shall change our vile body, that it may be fashioned like unto his glorious body, according to the working whereby he is able even to subdue all things unto himself" (Phi 3:20-21).

Between John's logical statement and Paul's exalted expectation scripture is absolutely insistent that we will be like Jesus Christ in our resurrection bodies. We have hinted at some features of our lives that may result from our likeness to Jesus, but we simply cannot predict all that this likeness will mean. Whatever details we do not know, however, we can summarize our likeness to Christ in several words:

Glorified

1Co 15:52 states that "In a moment, in the twinkling of an eye, at the last trump... the trumpet shall sound, and the dead shall be raised incorruptible, and we shall be changed." This moment of change will mark the receipt of our resurrection bodies. It is the moment that our journey from salvation to final redemption will be completed: "we all, with open face beholding as in a glass the glory of the Lord, are changed into the same image from glory to glory, even as by the Spirit of the Lord" (2Co 3:18).

Being glorified, whatever else it means, means incorruptible, better than we have ever been, and, while recognizable to one another, that none of us will be unattractive—even if any such concept will still exist.

Mobile

After his resurrection Jesus moved around during the forty days he was with his disciples. Where he was between the first Sunday he appeared to them and the next Sunday when he came again, we have no idea, but on that second occasion, he appeared to them behind locked doors with no difficulty. "Then came Jesus, the doors being shut, and stood in the midst, and said, Peace be unto you" (Joh 20:26). The disciples probably needed that greeting, as Jesus had simply appeared out of thin air. He appeared and disappeared at will, evidently not limited by time or space.

Our being like Jesus implies directly that we will have similar abilities. We won't need jets to go long distances, cars to go across town or cell phones to keep in touch!

Powerful

The implication of the entire picture of heavenly life, our likeness to Christ and the biblical concept of glorification and perfection leads us to a general conclusion that we will be powerful beyond our present capabilities.

Eating?

In all probability, the accounts of Jesus' meetings with his disciples on the beach (Joh 21:10, Luk 24:42), indicate that we will be free to eat, though it is likely we will not need to. The general tenor of biblical descriptions of our heavenly lives suggests that the "biology" of eternal life will be different. We may not need to eat; we may not have the same internal organs we have now; we may have no internal organs at all. But the scriptures speak of feasting and the supper of the Lamb (Rev 19:9), and fruits (Rev 22:2). Perhaps we will eat for pleasure without actually needing sustenance.

Our resurrection bodies may not need sleep. They probably won't, in fact, but we may choose to rest simply because it may be deliciously enjoyable.

Worship

The most exalted activity of our heavenly lives will be worshiping God. The twenty-four elders of Rev 4:10, however we interpret them, worship the Lord. Rev 15:4 says that "all nations will come and worship before thee." Rev 5:13 says, "every creature which is in heaven, and on the earth, and under the earth, and such as are in the sea, and all that are in them, heard me saying, Blessing, and honor, and glory, and power, be unto him that sitteth upon the throne, and unto the Lamb forever and ever." Worship is the superlative event of heavenly life.

We have already seen some glimpses of possible activities in the vast reality that will constitute the place of our eternal lives. However, to address directly a lingering impression that some people have about heaven, will we worship all the time? Is heaven to be spent standing with a congregation of saints and angels, actively worshiping God through praise, silence and song?

Here on earth, we are expected, even commanded, to worship the Lord, and we are told that we should not forsake the assembling of ourselves together with the church (Heb 10:25). Yet we do not spend all day, every day, in church. God doesn't expect that of us. He put us here to be active and to enjoy his creation. The first couple apparently had a daily time of communion with the Lord, but their lives consisted of various activities as they explored their environment, ate, spent time with each other, and experienced the world God had placed them in.

Nothing in the Bible says that we will worship all the time, not in the kind of focused event, whether ordered or spontaneous, that resembles going to church in this life. An informed student of the Bible may point to Rev 7:15, where John said, "Therefore are they before the throne of God, and serve him day and night in his temple: and he that sitteth on the throne shall dwell among them." The group being described consisted of tribulation saints, who while awaiting the resurrection, which in the vision would have been a very short time away, were in the heaven of heavens only. Only after the resurrection would they—will we—have the entire universe and re-created earth in which to live. These tribulation saints were pleased to be enjoying continuous worship, to inaugurate their own eternal lives, having come through such a time of turmoil and sacrifice.

From the picture gathered from all over the Bible, after the resurrection of saints, the judgment, and the reworking of creation, there will be worship freely and often. However, it would appear that there will be freedom to enjoy the many benefits of the new heaven and earth, interspersed with times of praise in the presence of God.

In addition, we might note that it will certainly be possible to be in a continuous state of worship no matter what we may be engaged in doing. Even in this world, people often comment that we may worship God while enjoying nature. Surrounded by the beauties of this world, we are often moved to private worship.

The author had an exhilarating experience of this kind of worship on a solo motorcycle trip across the United States. On a Sunday morning the planned ride was across the New Mexico desert. A text to the pastor back home said, "I am worshiping today in the Cathedral of the Desert Glory!" (The overuse of this concept as an excuse for not going to church does not lessen its truth!) When a Christian goes through a day filled with the Spirit, he is aware of the ability to commune with God and worship God while doing even mundane things. Surely in the heavenly life this combination of worship and activity will be in perfect continuum.

Service

It is often said that in heaven Christians will serve God forever. Many people who say this, asked what this service might involve, cannot elaborate. The service of worship will certainly be one activity, of course. Other than that, we would have difficulty speculating about specific tasks we might be given. We don't know what God needs doing!

Probably the best answer, however, is derived from looking at our lives here on earth. Christians are expected to serve the Lord always. If we look at our daily lives we might be tempted to wonder how some of our routine or mundane activities can be considered service to God, or even how some of the highlights of our years, such as wonderful vacations, can be called service. We do *disservice* to ourselves, however, if we fail to recognize that in this life as long as we are living in the flow of the Holy Spirit's leadership, whatever he leads us to do or *allows* us to pursue is part of our service to him. This will be no less true in the heavenly life. With no sinful impulses or temptations, all we do will be encompassed in the perfect inspiration of God's omnipresent Spirit. Therefore all we do will serve God.

God has not made us to be slaves, performing only laborious tasks. He has not made us even like the four living creatures around his throne, who do absolutely nothing but genuflect and gesticulate and offer exalted praise. God has made us human beings, finite creatures with curious minds and bodies made to experience a physical creation. He has made us relational beings who enjoy and need the companionship of others. He has made us creative and inventive. He has made us something *like himself,* because he made us in his image.

God's creative plan for us here has implications for our lives in heaven. We have no reason, scriptural or otherwise, to conclude that the kind of creatures we are now will be so changed in heaven that we will not resemble human beings. We must not conclude that serving God in heaven means being continual "gofers" performing menial tasks. Since we will be perfectly in harmony with him, whatever we do will be in his service.

Misconceptions. As a sidelight, we might also address a common idea in the culture (though not widespread among informed Christians) that people in heaven will either become angels or have wings like angels, wear white robes and play harps. This is a simplistic interpretation of several verses of scripture.

Rev 5:8 says that each of the twenty-four elders had a harp and sang a new song. This group of twenty-four is not representative of all the redeemed.

Rev 14:2 says that John heard a sound from heaven like rushing water and a peal of thunder, and that the sound was like harpists playing harps. Clearly this doesn't constitute a description of the activity of all the redeemed.

Rev 15:2 says that John saw those who had been victorious over the beast and that they held harps given them by God. This and the previous verse make clear that we as a heavenly congregation will make use of musical instruments in our worship, and probably many other things, since we will be creative in worshiping the Lamb and the Father.

There is a reference or two to our getting white robes (Rev 6:11, 7:9,13). There is no statement that even implies that we will always be wearing them. Many ministers acquire robes for use in church; they wear them on special occasions. The author is a judge and wears a robe in court, but not in the regular course of a day. Heaven's robes may be meant for formal worship and as such would be gladly donned for such occasions.

There is also nothing in the Bible about the redeemed getting wings. This particular assumption comes from connecting a mistaken interpretation of Jesus' statement in Mat 22:30 to a description of angels in Ezekiel's vision or in Rev 4:8. Nor does the Bible teach that any of us will have halos or become angels, even little children who die young. These are features of a popular cultural religion that merely resembles Christianity in some particulars.

As we have discovered, the Christian is privileged to look forward to a never-ending life of endless variety, discovery, enjoyment, fulfillment, peace, community, wholeness, and excitement. Taking what we have learned, we can imagine what it might be like to spend a day in the heavenly life. To that reasonable speculation we now turn.

9
A Day in Heaven

One morning, as the sun of the planet where you are currently spending time comes up, painting the sky with hues you never thought possible on earth, you gaze over the distant vista from a spacious and lofty deck and give thanks for such wonderment and glory in God's creation. The thought provokes worship, and you spread your arms and take in the beauty before you even as you call up the power of your resurrection body to transport yourself to the throne room of the Almighty.

In a flash of light you emerge into the vast, golden glow of the portico of the heaven of heavens, facing the indescribable crystalline structure in the New Jerusalem that is the location of the throne of God. Joining others who have brought themselves here, just as Jesus took himself place to place in Judea after his resurrection, you clasp hands with friends new and old, share smiles with everyone about the common joy that you all feel, and approach the throne room.

Entering the presence of the Lord in a wave of other worshipers, there is first a deep silence, as all see and feel the smile of God upon them, and he speaks to you in your heart, a message for you alone, as he is doing to every other person around you. It is a private word of his love. Your heart reaches out to God and expresses your adoration in response, and a fulness of joy and strength and peace wells up in you.

Spontaneously, you join the elders around the throne in song, you feel the surge of creative praise, and you make up a few verses of song yourself. On earth you were never creative, perhaps, but all that is behind you. It is natural and easy to sing a new song, give praise in a new way, express your heart to God in different strains, every time you come before his presence.

In these moments of worship no one keeps track of time, and you may be there a long while, standing in awe of God's holiness. Rising up from within you is a shudder of joy at your continuing eternal life because of the redemption of Jesus. Christ is upon his throne, merged in the bright glory before you with the brilliance of the everlasting Father. The Spirit surrounds everyone and pervades each worshiper.

After a chorus of shouts and a high note of praise, you sweep through the courtyard of the Lord and stroll in heavenly peace along the river of life, pausing to cup some of its water in your hands and enjoy its taste. A piece of fruit on one of the trees looks wonderful, and you eat it, remembering the apples and pears you ate before, and laughing at how infinitely better this fruit is. You are alive forever, and eating the fruit and drinking the water are both acts of worship as you acknowledge their glorious symbolism, and acts of pleasure made available to all the saints.

You spot a godly grandparent in the throng outside the throne room, and you glide through the other saints to her side, embracing her, even as she is embracing her own great-great-grandfather, whom you met just after the resurrection took place. How long ago was that? It seems like yesterday, so clear it is in your heavenly mind, yet so much has taken place since then.

Perhaps floating, flying, or just wishing yourself to the south gate of the city, you transport yourself through the portal and reappear on the flawless, verdant, healthy earth remade so recently after the judgment. Nothing of sin or its effects remains. A lion rubs against your leg and purrs. You pet him, tousling his mane and stroking his broad, muscular side. You greet a friend on his way to the gate you just left, carrying a new musical instrument he just crafted.

You enter a building, superbly built and wonderfully furnished, and you join friends and family members in the main room. Everybody is talking, and you join in. In a while, several of you decide to visit some of the new sites of the recreated earth. You simply speak the word or think the thought, and you are there.

The view is breathtaking. You saw the Grand Canyon or Niagara Falls or the Alps or one of hundreds of wonderful sights on the earth of your earlier life, but what lies before you now is different and surpassingly beautiful. As each of you quite naturally and freely utters a word of wonder to God and praises his handiwork, you move on to another beautiful setting, splash through a river, or hike up a mountain, never winded, never tired. You could ascend it by thought, but you walk for the sheer joy of it. Your body is a remarkable and perfect construction for your chosen activity, whatever it is.

Later in the day, you feel inspired to make something. You might even have an occupation of sorts—whatever appeals to you during that eon!—and you may pursue invention or exploration or art or music or design. Today your taste is art, and soon you have crafted an interesting work that you decide to take to someone who was a fast friend on earth. He has been exploring and staying on a distant planet, but it is of no consequence since you can be with him in a matter of moments by envisioning your destination. You take the "long" route, however, cruising through planets and stars in between, simply for the joy of imitating comets.

In the afternoon, at least what would be the afternoon on the re-created earth where you were this morning, the sweetness and stillness of a moment on a hillside cause you to rest and be content and motionless. You close your eyes, count your blessings one by one, acknowledge to the Holy Spirit inside you that you cannot finish the list, now or ever, and you laugh inside with inexpressible happiness at the thought.

After some time in revery, you open your eyes to the waning light of this planet, and the warmth of its sun makes you yearn to be in the Lord's direct presence, even though in the eternal realm his Spirit is more real than ever he was on earth when you strove daily to feel him within. In other words, you want to go to church!

So you take the express route back: you transport yourself by thought to the gate of heaven, and emerge into the bright, music filled holy city. You join a procession going in with great banners and a troupe of choristers entering with a well-rehearsed presentation of praise. The Lord hears and responds with a wave of warmth and a brilliant display of majesty, and he imparts thoughts of wisdom that bless every heart.

You want to speak with the Lord Jesus in this moment, and you make your way hastily toward his throne, as many others appear to be doing. As you near him, you are less and less aware of anyone else, until no one else is around you at all, just you and the Lord Jesus, who has stepped down from the throne and is standing with you, face to face. He is handsome and beautiful, and you feel such things in his presence that you cannot even describe. You reach for him, and he embraces you, and no joy on earth ever prepared you for the wholeness and peace you experience being with him.

You have a question for him. Perhaps it was one you always said you would ask God when you got to heaven. Perhaps it is something about the vast created order in which you now live. You ask him, he answers you, and your mind and heart are satisfied completely. Then you ask him, as you have before, why he loved you enough to die for you, and Jesus answers, Because I *AM* love. In the glow of his infinite smile, you step back from him, open your arms in praise and an expression of thanks, as he smiles you on your way.

Back in the throng milling about in the immense courtyards outside the glorious throne room, you see your earthly spouse. You have, in fact, seen each other, and you come near and wordlessly express your profound love. A touch and an embrace, and you are off, each to his planned fellowship of the evening.

Back on the new earth, you gather with a dozen or so friends in a mountainside cabin surrounded by picturesque woods and high meadows. You all share your day's experiences while perhaps unnecessarily dining on produce from a nearby, volunteer garden or sipping the juice of an orchard that grows spontaneously on the slopes. Into the night your laughter and excited stories go on, occasionally eliciting a word of praise to God from one and from all. The Holy Spirit fills the room and you bask silently in his rich presence.

When the sun is soon to be up, first one and then most of the gathered friends glide through the door and disappear into the predawn chill, going off to join family or friends elsewhere, near the start of another day. When all the friends have bid each other goodbye and left, you look up to see that a glimmering figure stands to the side of the room. You know him, because he identified himself shortly after the resurrection. He was the angel sent to you during your earthly life. He has come simply to see you and to tell you, in that almost indefinable angelic language that emanates from his entire form, that he is glad you are here, in the presence of the

Lord forever. He has told you that many times before. No sooner than you thank him for his ministering to you on earth, than he fades from view, no doubt returning to the fiery presence of God.

With that, you close your eyes and bask in the joy of your heavenly day. Behind your darkened eyelids comes the thought of a new expression of praise, and you begin planning your momentary transport to the throne of the Everlasting God, so that you may join with the worshiping throng and tell him how much you love him and how deeply you thank him for including you in his eternal people.

Who knows what will come in the day about to dawn? The answer is wonderfully obscured in expectancy.

> "However, as it is written: 'No eye has seen, no ear has heard, no mind has conceived what God has prepared for those who love him'" (1Co 2:9).

APPENDIX
ABBREVIATIONS OF BIBLE BOOKS

Gen	Genesis	Nah	Nahum
Exo	Exodus	Hab	Habakkuk
Lev	Leviticus	Zep	Zephaniah
Num	Numbers	Hag	Haggai
Deu	Deuteronomy	Zec	Zechariah
Jos	Joshua	Mal	Malachi
Jdg	Judges	Mat	Matthew
Rut	Ruth	Mar	Mark
1Sa	1 Samuel	Luk	Luke
2Sa	2 Samuel	Joh	John
1Ki	1 Kings	Act	Acts
2Ki	2 Kings	Rom	Romans
1Ch	1 Chronicles	1Co	1 Corinthians
2Ch	2 Chronicles	2Co	2 Corinthians
Ezr	Ezra	Gal	Galatians
Neh	Nehemiah	Eph	Ephesians
Est	Esther	Php	Philippians
Job	Job	Col	Colossians
Psa	Psalms	1Th	1 Thessalonians
Pro	Proverbs	2Th	2 Thessalonians
Ecc	Ecclesiastes	1Ti	1 Timothy
Sos	Song of Solomon	2Ti	2 Timothy
Isa	Isaiah	Tit	Titus
Jer	Jeremiah	Phm	Philemon
Lam	Lamentations	Heb	Hebrews
Eze	Ezekiel	Jam	James
Dan	Daniel	1Pe	1 Peter
Hos	Hosea	2Pe	2 Peter
Joe	Joel	1Jo	1 John
Amo	Amos	2Jo	2 John
Oba	Obadiah	3Jo	3 John
Jon	Jonah	Jde	Jude
Mic	Micah	Rev	Revelation

www.ingramcontent.com/pod-product-compliance
Lightning Source LLC
Chambersburg PA
CBHW051803040426
42446CB00007B/495